GETTING PAID *to Cruise*

SECRETS OF A PROFESSIONAL CRUISE HOST

Dream it!
Speak it!
Write it!
Live it!

CarolLee Miles

By CarolLee Miles

DISCLAIMER: The contents of this work are for informational purposes only. The author makes no warranty of any kind or nature whatsoever, and shall have no liability to any person, with respect to any particular result that may be realized from pursuing the concepts and ideas contained in this work. The ideas set forth are intended to provide the reader with an experience-based understanding of some of the more fundamental aspects of the role of Cruise Host.

The reader must bear in mind that the dynamics of every cruise will vary, dependent upon a number of variables including, but not limited to, the make-up of the customer group, applicable cruise line policies and regulations, the particular characteristics and amenities of the vessel, the personal dynamics of the cruise ship staff, the particular itinerary and dates of departure and return, and the local laws of the various destinations. These and numerous other circumstances must be considered in defining the Cruise Host duties and how they are to be performed.

As you set sail on your voyage of discovery, you must choose your own personal sailboat to success.

Peace Joy Publishing, LLC
P. O. Box 462454
Aurora, CO 80046-2044

Copyright © 2011 CarolLee Miles
All rights reserved.

ISBN: 1453644156
ISBN-13: 9781453644157
LCCN: 2010909917

ACKNOWLEDGMENTS

To Laura Pritchett, Editor, you nailed every point I tried to make with perfection – then brought the finished product to what it is today. Thank You!

To Dani Moore, thanks for bringing out the stories in me and believing in a vision … a vision of success.

To Brooke Shannon, for bringing the career of Cruise Hosting to light. You inspire me.

To my parents, Virginia and Walter Shannon, your constant encouragement to light up the world with joy is always in the background of my mind. I am so very proud to be your daughter. Your stars are forever near and I welcome our "Earth to Stars" conversations.

To our daughters, Traci and Terri, I acknowledge you and your families. I am so proud of everything you have become. You are both awesome mothers, a trait we all learned from Nannie. Wes and Michael, you give constant support to your crazy mother-in-law and I am grateful. Our four grandchildren, Blake, Natalie, Nina and Andie are a constant rejuvenating resource. In their words, "Nana, you ROCK!" Can you beat it?!

For the love and support of my sisters Shirley and Kay, I am grateful. Thanks to you, Jim and Ray, for telling me I should acknowledge there is a book in me. It is finally a reality, in part because you believe in me. Love you.

To my Ports of Call family, ITMI, WorldStrides, AAA Colorado and AAA Northern California families, thank you for giving me opportunities beyond all boundaries to travel and work as an 'Ambassador of Peace.' It has been quite a journey.

Ted and ITMI Staff, thanks for all you do in the world of tourism.

Eddie Wilson and all CD participants, you're awesome.

To Coach, Scott and Kim, for all your efforts in 'people helping people;' to Sandy, Shelly, and Stephanie for staying in touch and getting in touch; to Jeanie, Mary and Ron for your clear and concise information and sharing; to Juliet and ALL the directors who stayed the course; and to the entire YTB/ZamZuu family whose dreams consist of one big team, a huge THANKS to all for believing in my dream – a book that can help thousands with their careers.

And to those special women and men who stood by me in the most tender of times, may your hearts be filled with inspiration as you read this work. You have helped inspire and encourage this writing. You know who you are. Thank you from the bottom of my heart.

Last but not least a very special thank you to Larry Love. "You ROCK, too!"

TABLE OF CONTENTS

INTRODUCTION		xi
Why, Why, Why?		*xiii*
Secrets		*xiv*
PART I	**CRUISE HOST HANDBOOK 101**	1
CHAPTER 1	SOME BACKGROUND TRAVEL LINGO	3
CHAPTER 2	LOGISTICS OF OUR CRUISE	5
Pre-Cruise Calls		*5*
Documents		*7*
Travel Summary From Cruise Line		*8*
Shore Excursions Booked Online		*9*
EXERCISES		*10*
CHAPTER 3	PREPARING FOR THE CRUISE	11
Shuffling Paperwork/Forms/Details		*11*
Manifest		*12*
Guaranteed Cabins		*13*
Group Amenity Points (GAP)		*13*
Confidential Client Forms		*14*
Other Forms		*14*
Welcome-Farewell Party Invites/Note Cards		*15*
Door Decorations		*15*
Welcome Letters		*16*
Gifts		*17*
Supplies		*17*
Getting Paid		*18*
Wrap-Up Before the Cruise		*19*
EXERCISES		*20*
CHAPTER 4	EMBARKATION	21
Key Card/Cash-Free Cruising		*21*
Cabin		*22*

Ship Familiarization	23
Introduction to Ship Staff	25
EXERCISES	32

CHAPTER 5   SEA LEGS AND WELCOMES   33
Hospitality Desk   33
Door Decorations/Meeting Group   35
    EXERCISES   36

CHAPTER 6   GROUP ACTIVITIES ONBOARD   37
Welcome Party   37
Possible "Flow" of Welcome Party   39
Other Group Activities/Info Onboard   40
Repeat Passengers' Parties   41
Port Information   41
    EXERCISES   43

CHAPTER 7   ADDITIONAL KEY STAFF ONBOARD   45
Communication With Staff   47
    EXERCISES   47

CHAPTER 8   SHORE EXCURSIONS   49
King David Group Tour/Mazatlan   49
Other Shore Excursions   51
    EXERCISES   51

CHAPTER 9   ACCIDENT OR DEATH OF A CLIENT   53
Accident   53
Death of a Client   54
Checklist for Death   55
Disposition of the Body   56
Additional Considerations After Death   56
Remaining Group Members   57
Accident/Death Report   58
    EXERCISES   58

CHAPTER 10   TIPPING POLICIES   59
    EXERCISES   60

CHAPTER 11 FAREWELL PARTY	61
"Flow" of Farewell Party	62
Pre- or Post-Cruise Parties	62
EXERCISES	63
CHAPTER 12 DISEMBARKATION	65
Disembarkation Talk	65
Luggage Handling	66
Confirmation of Flights	67
Flight Arrangements	67
Disembarkation Procedures	69
EXERCISES	69
CHAPTER 13 PRE- OR POST-CRUISE EXTENSIONS	71
EXERCISES	72
CHAPTER 14 THE TRIP HOME	73
Reports and Forms – More Papers, Papers, Papers	73
Expense Report	73
Over-All Recap	74
Thank You Notes	75
EXERCISES	75
EXAM	**76**
SUMMARY	**76**
WHAT'S NEXT?	**77**
PHOTO GALLERY	**79**

PART II		**WANDERLUST MEANDERINGS**	**103**
CHAPTER 1		SECRETS BEHIND THE BOOK	105
	EXERCISES		*106*
CHAPTER 2		MY WANDERLUST CAREER	107
	EXERCISES		*108*
CHAPTER 3		PORTS OF CALL TRAVEL CLUB	109
	EXERCISES		*115*
CHAPTER 4		FINDING A PURPOSE IN MY LIFE	117
	EXERCISES		*119*
CHAPTER 5		THE END OF POC; FINDING OTHER AVENUES	121
	EXERCISES		*125*
CHAPTER 6		CASE STUDY #1 - ITMI	127
	EXERCISES		*131*

PART III – FEAR OF CAREER CHANGE			**133**
CHAPTER 1		ADDRESSING FEARS	135
CHAPTER 2		SECRETS OF CAREER CHANGE	137
	EXERCISES		*140*
CHAPTER 3		F-E-A-R	141
	EXERCISES		*144*
CHAPTER 4		REPLACING F-E-A-R WITH L-O-V-E	145
	EXERCISES		*147*
CHAPTER 5		A FORMULA FOR FEAR	149
	EXERCISES		*152*

CHAPTER 6	WHAT IS THE SECRET IN FACING FEAR	153
Case Study #2, YTB/ZamZuu		*154*
EXERCISES		*166*

CHAPTER 7	THE INTERNET AND PROFESSIONAL CRUISE HOSTS	167
EXERCISES		*168*

PART IV – SECRETS OF CRUISE HOST PSYCHOLOGY 169

CHAPTER 1	SHARING STORIES	171
EXERCISES		*172*

CHAPTER 2	A TRUE FATHER AND SON STORY	173
EXERCISES		*175*

CHAPTER 3	CHALLENGING CLIENTS	177
EXERCISES		*179*

CHAPTER 4	SECRET MODEL FOR CONFLICT CONFRONTATION	181
EXERCISES		*185*

CHAPTER 5	USING THE SECRET "MODEL"	187
EXERCISES		*189*

PART V – SECRETS OF CRUISING INTO THE FUTURE 191

CHAPTER 1	A JOURNEY OF PEACE	193
Surprise Bombs, Physical And Mental		*195*
EXERCISES		*198*

CHAPTER 2	A CD ENTITLED 'PEACE'	199
EXERCISES		*202*

CHAPTER 3 CHANGING LIVES	203
EXERCISES	*204*
CHAPTER 4 BUILDING A FUTURE WITH PEACE	205
EXERCISES	*208*
CHAPTER 5 WRITING MY SONG/SINGING YOURS	209
EXERCISES	*210*
CHAPTER 6 THE SECRET OF YOUR SUCCESS	211
EXERCISES	*211*

SUMMARY   212

HELPFUL RESOURCES   213

THE PEACE CD   215

ABOUT THE AUTHOR   217

INTRODUCTION

Welcome to the cruise world! And what a world it is. During the last few years it has been quite common to turn on the news and see yet another new cruise ship taking her maiden voyage. Cruise line after cruise line reported "bigger and better." Even with the depressed economy, more new ships are still being introduced in the marketplace. This year, six more brand new ships are scheduled to make their debut.

The Associated Press recently reported for the next nineteen years 10,000 Baby Boomers a day will turn 65. These societal changes will determine retirement possibilities. Some of the 10,000 a day may be ready to retire and start traveling more, while some may be suddenly looking for a new career because they cannot afford to retire. Those numbers are significant when thinking about the cruise world in general.

The cruise industry is growing at amazing speed, similarly to the Electronic world -- more specifically the Internet travel world and the Social Networking world. Why?

Travel is the largest industry on the planet and cruise lines are capturing a magnanimous market-share. If we stop and investigate why this is happening, the answers become clear. Cruising is the best bargain out there in over-all vacations, and prices have been at an all-time low as deep discounts respond to the mounting competition.

Competition in the cruise industry keeps prices down, services top notch, entertainment spectacular, food preparation and presentation exquisite, significant amenities flowing for past cruisers, new and innovative activities onboard, and airfare free or 2-for-1 pricing commonplace. When you consider all you get for one price, it is like no-holds-barred luxury at its best.

Years ago, when cruises first emerged, there was a special energy that involved connecting man, land and sea. A different sort of energy is found today – because of the Internet. Now it's possible to make vacation plans on the Internet, including a three-day cruise, a more extensive Around the World Voyage, or anything in between.

To summarize, cruising is timely, profitable, fun, and has a strong future. Want to be a part of it? If you've picked up this book, you probably do – and I must say it has been one of the most rewarding, amazing and exciting experiences of my life. In this book, we will explore some options in the world of cruising. I will show you the in's and out's of the industry – the things no one else will tell you.

So: if you're looking for exciting opportunities, stay tuned (and as a side note, you may find yourself exploring options in other careers as well.)

"Getting Paid to Cruise: Secrets of a Professional Cruise Host" primarily focuses on:

- *Professional Tour Directors/Cruise Hosts who want to specialize in cruises,*
- *Travel agents and referring travel agents who have discovered hundreds of cruises from which they can sell and reap profits,*
- *New internet travel site owners who are looking for innovative ways to serve their clients better,*
- *Cruise lines that want to better serve their clients by working with the professional Cruise Host to keep passengers coming back for more,*
- *Individuals who are willing to open up their creative juices to search for their perfect career,*
- *Innovative and forward-thinking individuals who want to live their passion and find their calling,*
- *Those who are looking for training in the field of Cruise Hosting.*

"Getting Paid to Cruise: Secrets of a Professional Cruise Host" focuses on large cruise ships.   There are various terms that are often used -- the cruise escort might be called Cruise Host, Tour

Director, Tour Manager, Tour Conductor, or Tour Escort. For simplicity here, the travel professional to whom I refer is called a Cruise Host.

WHY, WHY, WHY?

Why read this book? There are many reasons, none-the-least of which is, you may be looking for change. You can become a more knowledgeable professional in the field of cruise hosting while working **for** a Tour Operator. Or by **being** a Tour Operator, you can pride yourself in having additional information that allows you to perform more professionally for your clients. Here are points to consider:

1. You can offer expert advice because you know how to "explore the ship and understand who runs it," saving clients' **time** and **money** on their cruise vacation.
2. You can offer suggestions for booking as well as saving time in exploring on land because you have either traveled there yourself or researched possible activities while the ship is in port.
3. You can take advantage of travel discounts while educating yourself on various cruise lines.
4. If you know how to throw a good party, you're in luck. Parties can be an integral part of the cruise experience.
5. You can take hands-on training (free if you are a travel agent or travel site owner who has passed a series of training classes) with cruise lines that offer the possibility of free cruises in order to become an "expert" on their product. (Now is that enticing or what?)
6. You can help others by becoming an Ambassador of Peace. This includes the psychology of handling conflict as well as the international diplomat role of interacting peacefully with other nations. It's all about people helping people. I love that.

When "Getting Paid to Cruise" first started gestating in my mind, I was writing a manual about my profession as a Cruise Host. The finished product, however, includes a whole lot more. Combining some personal stories and memoirs brought the book more positive energy and a more complete story.

Yes, it is possible to do what I have done for the past 25 years and get paid for it. Yes, it can be a career in today's world. Yes, you can travel the world with the absolute wanderlust that is born in some of us. And yes, if you are looking for a career change or simply interested in cruising for one reason or another, this book may indeed light up your life.

I am a professional Cruise Host that escorts groups all over the world, living and working with them to experience their dreams of a lifetime. In four short years after I found my dream job in 1986, I had stepped foot on all seven continents. Today I have traveled in over 100 countries and that includes taking cruises galore.

I don't live on cruise ships as part of the crew (though they do share an occasional party with me) or work for a particular cruise line. The view from my office window changes every day I work. I get to wear casual clothes and tennis shoes, but I also love wearing my Red Carpet cocktail dress when the occasion presents itself.

My pay varies, but the real benefit has been the incredible people I meet on land and sea, as well as the back alleys of third world countries. Those precious relationships are safely tucked away in the corners of my mind and cannot be given a monetary value.

My wealth is immeasurable because I could never put a dollar value on the education received from the simplest of exchanges in many different corners of the world. In that regard I am a billionaire a billion times over. In short: I love my job.

SECRETS

This book contains many practical components, including some of my secrets I am willing to share. The first piece of advice is to love yourself because you deserve it. The second is for you to consider creating a way to help others as you follow your dreams. Stated simply: as you give, you will receive.

After each chapter, investigative-type questions will help you explore your own secrets, including reflections on your past, present and future. Inter-active exercises will start your creative juices.

Diagnosing various events from your circumstances may help you arrive at your destination of getting the job you want, improving the job you have or thinking of other opportunities for employment. That might be called your future.

Examine your past. Explore your present. Envision your future. Enrich your fortune. Consider this a joyous time to embrace abundance. Make it a fun adventure. Your particular calling awaits you in a world with outstretched arms. But guess what? Only you can identify that calling. Only you can visualize what that calling looks and feels like because "it" is inside of **you**.

Some of my personal secrets are used in the book to help you understand my quest for finding an occupation that fulfills some of my passions in life. When I found a job that felt more like play than work, I knew I had found a good place for me. I want the same for you.

You can actually apply these techniques to any quest for the need to feel more whole or complete, especially as it relates to occupation.

As you'll read, you'll see that one of my case studies involves two men who started a company because of the joy they both exhibited in their love of Tour Directing. This particular company changed my life in more ways than one and continues to give me new opportunities in my field. Associations such as this are invaluable in anyone's career field.

Envision a friend who has been successful in doing what they love to do. Now picture yourself in your own perfect scenario by comparison. Your own vision is your greatest roadmap to success. Hold that vision close to your heart. Love it. Let it grow. Setting the path is only the beginning. Dream it! Speak it! Write it! Live it!

We will also examine another case study about a man who received a vision from his mother when he was sixteen years of age. With his two co-founders, he did not stop until the vision came to fruition. Perhaps you might know other success stories you can add to your own memoirs.

For years I have been told *"You are so lucky! You get to vacation all the time."* I usually smile and think to myself *"And you don't know the half of it."*

L-U-C-K, simply translated, has taken on a new meaning for me: <u>L</u>ove <u>U</u>ntil <u>C</u>reation <u>K</u>nocks. This definition of L-U-C-K could be described as my life's journey. My mom and wife roles played the Love part while I waited for Cruise Hosting (the Creation part) to knock. However, the profession did not magically fall into my lap. I had to work at making it happen.

Life is too short to be unhappy as you cruise through life on land or at sea, doing whatever you're doing in any kind of career. My wish for you is to embrace a new joy, the joy of discovery as we venture out together. I encourage you to try using my L-U-C-K philosophy to pave your way.

I am inviting you to go on a cruise with me because now living in the *mature* stage of my life (that stage teenagers call 'what could Grandma possibly know anyway?') I can share some experiences that happened along the way of gathering these visible wrinkles. I have in fact learned some practical *and* some philosophical lessons about life – and I think they will be of value to you.

First of all I suggest you keep an open mind, keep a pen and paper close by, and make notes. I am hoping you'll be encouraged to write down what you want to get from this book, followed by how you plan to achieve your own success. This mental journey could lead you to **your destination.** The plan is to make **your** dreams come true.

How you define success is totally up to you. My definition of success is all about finding inner peace and looking for ways to be of service. When you learn to live from the heart, give with commitment and purpose plus find your truth, you will not have to worry about your business flourishing. If you simply continue to give, your business will be paying it forward, so to speak. And you will find contentment.

Has your "appetite" for a new career been whetted? Is your brain turning flip-flops for new possibilities in the marketplace?

If the answer is YES, then let's get started. The book is divided into several parts. Part I is a practical guide which is directed toward the Cruise Host – what one does (1) in preparation for the cruise, (2) from the time he/she gets on the ship with a group and (3) until it's time to depart and return home. The remaining Parts II, III, IV, and V explore lessons, psychology, stories and various wisdoms gleaned from my 25+ years in the travel industry. In short, this book will be of practical value, but also offer insider tips to consider all along your pathway of life.

Now don your life vest! We're about to cast off in a sea of adventure.

PART 1

∽

CRUISE HOST HANDBOOK 101

CHAPTER 1

SOME BACKGROUND TRAVEL LINGO

Before we delve in, it's important to set up some basic "lingo" you may find used in the travel/cruise world of today.

"Brick and Mortar" Travel Agency: Usually in an office type atmosphere, the agency may have one or more travel agents who may or may not accompany groups when booked through the agency.

Home-based Travel Agents: Having completed and passed all necessary Travel Agent classes and accreditation, these professionals hold the title of Travel Agent. They may operate individually as their own company or they may be a home-based agent for a larger travel company.

Tour Operator: A Tour Operator is a company that puts together group tours or cruises to be sold to the public. Either of the above examples could also be called a Tour Operator because they are in the business of selling cruises and tours.

Professional Cruise Host: Hired by a Tour Operator or Travel Agency to escort a group on a cruise ship. She/he might also be called a Cruise or Tour Escort, Tour Conductor, Tour Director, or other term defined by the Tour Operator. Note that cruise lines use TC for Tour Conductor.

In this book, the term Professional Cruise Host or simply Cruise Host is used.

In either of the above businesses, you might consider yourself a professional Cruise Host. After all, you could be seen as the travel professional representing a company that strives to provide a service where the clients enjoy the following benefits:

- Get the most value for their money.
- Expect good communication.
- Understand that your knowledge of the industry places them in top priority status with the cruise line on which you are traveling.
- Know they will get special attention.
- Understand someone is always looking out for the best interest of the group.
- Want to travel with you again because of your professionalism.
- Receive first-class service from a first-class personality.
- Are proud to recommend you to their friends.

Pied Piper. Person designated as group leader who organizes group or in part carries out some logistical responsibilities with the group. This person might also benefit from parts of this material.

As you read and digest my way of performing professionally as a Cruise Host, start to formulate a plan of your own. Nothing is set in stone. It's up to you as to how you handle your own group(s).

In exploring a pretend Mexican Riviera cruise, I only go into detail about those on the cruise staff that will be the most helpful to you as you carry out your job. You will be exposed to many more officers and staff on cruise ships that do their job extremely well. Feel free to add them into your own thoughts and plans as you travel on different cruise lines on various ships. Note also titles of ship staff may vary from cruise line to cruise line.

CHAPTER 2

LOGISTICS OF OUR CRUISE

The first thing to do is gain a basic understanding of logistics and things to think about. Pretend that I am hired by a Tour Operator, CLMPeace Travel, and my contact tells me it is a very important group that is returning for their third cruise with the company. We want to keep them happy. We are traveling on Holland America Line's *Oosterdam*, visiting Cabo, Mazatlan and Puerto Vallarta on our Mexican Riviera cruise.

My Tour Operator has arranged a special group Shore Excursion in Mazatlan with King David Tours that I will host. (That's great because I know King David personally. He has owned and operated a private tour company for many years, is dependable and fun, his staff is great and past groups rave about this excursion.) There will also be two parties on the ship to host -- one to welcome guests and one as a farewell. I will host a Hospitality Desk, hours to be posted.

Clients have received a personalized nametag and will receive a gift onboard (alarm clock – one per single or one per couple) and a $50 per cabin shipboard credit. Alarm clocks are to be shipped to the dock and will come to my cabin in one box. I am to get information on how they are to be shipped.

PRE-CRUISE CALLS

She would also like me to make a pre-cruise call to all the clients. (I like this special request. After you have done a few last-minute calls to clients, you realize how that extra attention sets the stage for a cooperative effort all the way around. Clients love this.)

Keep in mind, however, not all Tour Operators have their Cruise Host make the pre-cruise call. If hired by a Tour Operator, you carry out the duties assigned to you. If you decide to make a suggestion to a Tour Operator such as pre-tour calls, be sure and be tactful in the way you approach the subject.

Have your reasons for calling clear in your mind. Here are some of my reasons:

1. Getting acquainted pre-cruise by phone makes the client feel as though they know you personally.
2. Clients feel you are genuinely concerned about their well being from beginning to end of the trip.
3. If there are questions or concerns about logistics of the trip, clients can talk those through and feel more at ease when starting their journey.
4. If there are special needs or physical challenges, you become more aware of the exact nature of those potential problems ahead of time instead of last minute with the entire group present.
5. Those who have not taken a cruise before are especially appreciative for your knowledge about logistics of day-to-day activities onboard a ship.
6. Clients feel more a part of a group when they can ask about the group size, such things as where most are from, etc. As a Cruise Host, one goal is to keep the group interactive with each other and with you.
7. You begin to build a confidence level in your ability to handle the group with professional ease.
8. You will find clients generally have questions about shore excursions. Remember on our cruise the Tour Operator is including a King David Tour in Mazatlan. Be sure and mention the included tour to the clients and answer any questions they may have about logistics.

    Some clients may not be planning to do any other excursion but the included one. It is essential you have all pertinent information about the included group tour when you speak to the clients.

If a question comes up you cannot answer, get back to the Tour Operator for more detail so you can be clear. It is perfectly OK to say you do not have an answer as long as you tell the client you will try and find out and get back to them as soon as possible.

(More information on shore excursions later.)
9. The phone call generally makes the clients eager to meet you as they feel your excitement about the trip.

If you are the Tour Operator and have arranged your own group, you may find last-minute calls to clients are also a good plan. Making each client feel special is part of making the group experience successful. It is also a good reason they will want to book with you again.

DOCUMENTS

"I'm so excited! I'm so excited!"
"My doc-u-ments arrived and I'm DELIGHTED!"

Whether one receives cruise documents by e-mail or by regular mail, an excitement fills the air while the reality of the upcoming cruise sets in. If the client has been on 1 or 100 cruises, the feeling of adventure starts to mount while reading through the information. As the professional Cruise Host, the same is true for **you**.

If documents are mailed, clients usually get them 2-3 weeks before departure. Mailed cruise documents and information usually come in a rectangular shaped booklet with tear-out voucher pages and other pertinent information.

If documents are e-mailed (it's the 'green' thing to do these days), pages of information will be printed off to reveal the details of the cruise. These are not quite as exciting, but certainly serve the purpose.

Once confirmed on a cruise, clients receive an identification number. With that number they can go online and fill out necessary pre-embarkation forms. Cruise lines require the information before boarding.

Clients will also use this ID number to schedule their Shore Excursions online if they want to book before embarkation day. They can book on the ship as well, but usually lines are long -- so there are advantages to booking ahead.

TRAVEL SUMMARY FROM CRUISE LINE

In getting prepared for my cruise, the next thing I take time to consider are the following items on my own travel summary so I am familiar with the various pieces of information in case questions arise:

1. Cruise Summary booking number.
2. Passengers' names & ages on the booking.
3. Passenger status with cruise line & member number.
4. Insurance information (if booked insurance). Some may take cruise line; some may take Tour Operator insurance.
5. Air travel information (if booked through the cruise line).
6. Ship name, voyage number, number of nights.
7. Destination; i.e. Mexican Riviera or Panama Canal.
8. Embarkation port and date.
9. Disembarkation port and date.
10. Cabin number or GUARANTEE & Category. (More discussion on GUARANTEE later.)
11. Identification # for the cruise or cruise/tour.
12. Onboard currency (how folio will be charged).
13. Note: This is usually US dollars.
14. Boarding time and departure time.
15. Information to contact the ship in case of unforeseen delays on departure days.
16. Dated itinerary with hours in each port and pertinent information regarding the port (such as limited wheelchair access, tender required, etc.)
17. Itinerary dress code: For example, 2 casual nights, 2 formal nights and 3 business casual nights.
18. Documents needed (passport/visa requirements).
19. Luggage tags.
20. Emergency notification information.
21. Transfer tickets if in package (from airport to ship, ship to airport).
22. Spa services information.
23. Shore excursion information.

SHORE EXCURSIONS BOOKED ONLINE

On this trip, I'm aware it is not necessary to have detailed information for every shore excursion offered on the ship, but certainly have an over-all working knowledge of the types of things being offered.

Do keep in mind there is a code for various levels of physical ability printed in the informational material for Shore Excursions. I keep those parameters in mind when I know a client is recovering from knee surgery, is confined to a wheelchair, or is using a walker or oxygen, for example.

It is very important to know what the various "codes" represent. That will be spelled out in the information, but sometimes you have to look for it.

Always be aware recommendations from you could influence a client's decision; therefore it is best for them to make up their own mind. Some ninety-year-olds are perfectly capable of doing the Zip Line while others simply are not in that kind of physical shape.

Quite often I am asked something like "What would you recommend I do as a Shore Excursion in Cabo?" My standard answer is: "That all depends on what your interests are, how much money you want to spend and how much time you want to spend with a group versus on your own exploring. I'm sure you will come up with the answer after you have a chance to look through all the details of what might interest you."

If I know certain Shore Excursions are likely to sell out, I do encourage them to book early to hold a space. For example, if the helicopter ride in Alaska is the whole purpose for their trip, make sure they understand they need to take every precaution to secure tickets by signing up early.

Often you will be asked the question, "Are there cheaper tours offered at the dock?" The answer to that question is "**Usually yes; however there are risks involved.**"

For example, I might say: "If a tour purchased through the ship is delayed, the cruise ship will wait for the tour to return. If the private taxi has a flat tire and clients are delayed in returning for departure, they may find the cruise ship has already departed. The crew may be waving goodbye as the ship leaves the port. Oops! See you at the next stop!"

EXERCISES

1. How can you relate to the material in this chapter?
2. Have you cruised before?
3. How did the feeling of getting the documents affect your anticipation of the cruise (a) if you have cruised or (b) if you have not cruised before?
4. What are your thoughts on pre-cruise calls?

CHAPTER 3

PREPARING FOR THE CRUISE

Time spent in preparation for the cruise is essential. I've learned life will be a lot easier onboard when I'm organized about details of the trip ahead of time.

SHUFFLING PAPERWORK/FORMS/DETAILS

Oh yes! No matter the business, there is always the task of dealing with those necessary papers. Although 'green' is in, some details are important in paper form if I'm (1) keeping clients' best interests in mind and (2) keeping ship staff current with information about your group.

In this case, CLMPeace Travel is going to provide me with information about the cruise and participants. That information most probably will include such things as:

- Cruise line and ship name, cruise dates
- Clients name, address, phone number
- Booking number
- Category of cabin paid for
- Cabin number assigned or guaranteed
- Name(s) of all clients in each cabin
- Total cost of the cruise per client
- Flight information with any deviation noted
- Insurance paid for or declined (cruise line or company)

- Extra amenities contracted for with detail (For example $50 per cabin or $50 per person shipboard credit – there might be 3 in cabin; welcome and farewell party details, etc.)
- Info on celebrations while on board
- Who, if anyone, clients are traveling with (and cross reference to those clients/cabins.)
- Specific dining requests (For example, Early seating, Table for 8, request seating with *friends names*. Another example, Open Seating or Anytime Dining.)
- Physical limitations if known
- Cruise line repeat passenger if known
- Pre- or post-cruise tours (extended tours clients have booked and detail – more info on this later)
- Gift information and distribution detail (For example, 1 travel alarm per couple or per person)

Now wouldn't it be great if there was some form to kind of summarize all the pertinent information we'll need for ship personnel? Indeed, we just happen to have such a document. We call it a Passenger Manifest or quite simply Manifest for short.

MANIFEST

My group manifest will come from CLMPeace Travel. It has details to be shared with various departments on the ship in a clear and concise statement.

The Cruise Host's name is clearly marked for contact if someone in the group has a problem. You can find an example of the group manifest for our cruise at www.CarolLeeMiles.com – Book/Forms.

Additionally we will receive detail about such things as pre-arranged and confirmed cocktail parties including the rate per person that will be charged and how it is paid, information about a hospitality desk if pre-arranged, amenities included or not (see GAP point discussion in the next section). Forms for finalizing detail are provided by the cruise line.

It is always a good practice to take along a copy of all paperwork, contracts, etc., when traveling with a group. Keep good notes to document interaction with the Tour Operator or directly with the cruise line. Record points in the conversation and the date. Every detail documented helps continue to establish a good reputation with a particular cruise line and staff.

When making a manifest as a Tour Operator, keep in mind clear and concise information helps. When the Tour Operator provides the manifest (as is our case here), it is designed with the information they feel is important. Items will vary from cruise to cruise, depending on the itinerary, if it is a cruise/tour (land tour included pre- or post-cruise or both), etc.

GUARANTEED CABINS

If a cabin is marked "GUARANTEE" on the Manifest, the cruise line is guaranteeing a certain cabin type and category, dependent on what the client has paid for. The client is guaranteed to get a cabin at least as good as the category he/she paid for and **may** even get a better cabin for the same price.

The Tour Operator will try to get the Guaranteed cabin(s) converted to an actual cabin number before the cruise departs. In rare cases, the Guarantee will be converted at the dock upon check-in. I always assure the client this happens all the time and cruise lines are very good about assigning the same or better category before departure. It is a Guarantee this will happen.

GAP POINTS

Group Amenity Points (GAP) are points assigned to the Tour Operator when the group is booked. The number of points assigned to the group is dependent on such factors as how early before cruise departure the group is booked and how large the group is, for example.

Points might be used toward cocktail parties, gifts, onboard credit or Tour Conductor credits dependent upon what agreements are made between the Tour Operator and the cruise line. Those details will be agreed upon in the final interaction with the cruise line.

Additionally the Tour Operator may be responsible for paying the charges for an additional cocktail party, a bottle of wine in the cabin on arrival or whatever the company chooses to do. Details for all charges should be spelled out in the paperwork – mine is clear as I assemble the details ready to take.

CONFIDENTIAL CLIENT FORMS
(example found at www.CarolLeeMiles.com – Book/Forms.)

In the past, a Tour Operator would tend to provide a very comprehensive client information form. However with the privacy laws and concerns of today, these type forms are sometimes not quite as extensive or invasive.

The form may simply ask for Name, Address, Phone, E-mail address, celebrations while onboard and who to contact in the case of an emergency. Additionally, the form might have a space for medical information IF the client wants to volunteer that information. It is up to the Tour Operator to decide on the content of such forms.

OTHER FORMS

CLMPeace Travel does not have specific forms to fill out except for an expense report that documents expenditures with receipts. (We like fewer forms so this is good.)

There will be more information on handling expenses at the end of our cruise. For now just keep in mind an expense reconciliation is important. Remember to keep ALL receipts. Personally I keep all these together in one envelope from beginning to end of the trip.

Some Tour Operators might require the Cruise Host to distribute a client end-of-cruise form to obtain feedback. If so they will provide such forms and give directions on how to handle distributing them.

CLMPeace Travel simply likes a written overview of the cruise with any pertinent information the Cruise Host thinks would be good to improve services. This type report is simple, easy and covers the important bases.

I like this "less is good" style of operation. However I cooperate with a Tour Operator with whatever forms they require. Their requirements dictate my interaction when necessary to fulfill my duties while representing their company.

WELCOME-FAREWELL PARTY INVITES/NOTE CARDS

CLMPeace Travel has their own invitations for the parties. A Tour Operator may or may not want their own logo on everything written that goes to their clients while onboard.

Pre-printed party invitations are a risk at best. The reason is the Tour Operator may have made arrangements for the parties with someone in the cruise line office, but when the Cruise Host gets onboard with the group a last-minute change may be necessary because of unforeseen schedule conflicts. If pre-printed invitations are used, definitely take a supply of blank ones just in case. That way all bases are covered.

Blank note cards (with Tour Operator logo on them) are good to have along. Ask the Tour Operator contact for a supply. If you are the Tour Operator, you may want to consider investing in a product like this. They come in handy for last-minute updates on many occasions.

I also keep personalized note cards with me as a back-up. They can be ordered online or from an office supply or stationery store. A favorite of mine is www.AmericanStationery.com/catalog.

DOOR DECORATIONS

Cabin door decorations are a good source of free advertisement plus a decorated door is a nice "Welcome" from the Cruise Host. NOTE: Make sure you check onboard (usually the Purser's Desk or Passenger Services Representative) to make sure it is okay to put signs on the doors before you put them up.

The sky is the limit as far as what you want to put on the door. Generic "party" paper from any office supply store can be used festively. If you are a creative design type and good at computer skills, you may want to design your own. These are always a hit.

Note: Because of time limitations on the first day boarding the ship, sometimes I decorate doors after clients have retired for their first night onboard. This is perfectly acceptable. **In the Welcome Letter I like to suggest they leave the signs on the door for the entire cruise.**

Reasons for leaving them on the doors include:

- Free advertisement for the Tour Operator.
- Cause for discussion with nearby cabin occupants.
- Easy visual distinction in case I am putting any additional information under their door.
- A cheerful, personal "hello" from me every time they go to their cabin.
- Ease of delivery for cabin attendants when gifts are being delivered for the group.

WELCOME LETTERS

Generally a friendly welcome letter or letter of introduction regarding the Cruise Host can serve several purposes. It will come:

(1) From the Tour Operator through the mail or e-mail,
(2) From the Tour Operator but delivered by the Cruise Host on the ship or
(3) From the Cruise Host personally and delivered on the ship.

If you are the Tour Operator and traveling with the group, you may ask "Why would I also do a welcome letter when we get onboard?" The answer is simple. The client has everything right in front of him/her that pertains to the information you want shared.

It also negates the statement(s) that are made quite frequently like "You never told us that." Or "You said we would have information from you when we get onboard." Or "How can you expect me to remember everything?"

If the Tour Operator sends out the Welcome Letter from you in advance of the cruise, a picture of you is nice to include. The client will then (1) know who you are when they see you in an airport/

cruise terminal/onboard and (2) If you do a pre-cruise call, the client can actually put a "face to a name" while hearing the Cruise Host voice. It's a good thing.

GIFTS

Nothing pleases me more than to be the one presenting gifts on the cruise ship if (when) they are provided. Doesn't everyone love to receive a gift?

All Tour Operators do not give gifts, but you might think about it. A gift gives a good "return on investment" with the client. Members of groups I have been with in the past continue to rave about certain gifts received before, during or after a cruise.

When clients come to breakfast or lunch with a logo-infused "brand," it causes questions and excited enthusiasm ensues. It's talk about an agency. An around-the-neck nametag with company name on the front, pockets for storing key cards, credit cards, etc., is not only functional, but it does what? It draws attention to a brand. A small pair of binoculars does the same.

Even for the small Tour Operator, creating a clientele takes some ingenuity. Other options might include little personal gifts along the way, but that gets cumbersome and can be expensive in the long run.

SUPPLIES

You can pretend you are off to school when you pack your "supplies" for your group. Items that might be included are:

- Scissors
- Stapler
- Curly ribbon
- Colored marking pens
- Letterhead
- Notes with letterhead and/or personalized
- Scotch tape
- Balloons

- Hole punch
- White out
- Glue
- Paper clips
- Rubber bands
- Notebook for Hospitality Desk
- Sign for Hospitality Desk
- Note pad for cabin door
- For birthdays and anniversaries, retirements, etc., you can use your own imagination to make the celebration FUN! Cards, balloons and door decorations are good.

I cannot tell you how many times I've used a round tube of curly ribbon. This little gem comes in handy more than any other item because it can be used for so many things. Curly ribbon can tie up gifts, decorate a door, attach to a simple birthday card, be used for a gag gift, be used around a special photo you purchase for a guest and many other things. Trust me on this one.

Cruise lines should not be expected to copy a lot of your material as handouts. Paper is costly and the information is coming from **you**, not the cruise line. If I have handouts and the group is small, I carry them with me. The same is true for games. If you do ask the cruise line to make some copies for you, expect that you will be charged for the service.

Having games or puzzles with a theme tied to the itinerary can add to the cruise experience. A game can be used as an icebreaker at a welcome party to get to know others in the group or a way to stay in contact on cruise days. With a short itinerary such as ours (only 7 days), games are not as pertinent as perhaps a 14-day cruise with lots of days at sea. That is when they really come in handy.

GETTING PAID

On our pretend cruise I am considered an "Independent Contractor" and I will be paid for this cruise and this cruise alone. I will not receive any employee-type benefits and I agree to promote the company in any way I can within professional reason while on the ship.

The amount the Cruise Host is paid per day can vary from Tour Operator to Tour Operator, depending on the situation, group size, what type group it is, etc. CLMPeace Travel has agreed to pay me $75 per day in salary plus any expenses incurred because it's a small group. In this case I will be paid up front for the salary and I will also receive a check for estimated expenses. Pay could range from $75 to $150 or $200 per day, depending on the circumstances, itinerary, group size, group activities, number of Cruise Hosts, etc.

For estimated expenses, they sent me a check for $800. I am to use this money for automatic gratuities of $10 per day which will be charged to my cabin bill, tips of $2 per person for each of the two parties involved, small gifts at group parties, personal expenses for transportation to/from the airport, tips for luggage at the airport and cruise terminal, taxi fares, etc.

We agree before the trip any charges I incur will be documented with receipts on an expense report at the end of the trip, a final reconciliation will be made and we will settle the difference as soon as possible after completion of the trip. This is perfectly acceptable and in accordance with the way in which expenses are handled with the other companies I have worked for in the past.

I am also asked to keep in contact by ship Internet service. Because we do not know the rate that will be charged at this time, I agree to expense it back and keep the cost to a minimum by communicating only when I feel it is necessary to do so. (Ship Internet charges can be quite costly, and I routinely use Internet Cafes on land when I can in order to keep ship costs to a minimum.)

WRAP-UP BEFORE THE CRUISE

My contact at CLMPeace Travel called and we have agreed on all details for the trip, the pre-tour calls are made, the suitcases are packed and now it's time to start our journey together. Let the good times roll!

EXERCISES

1. What would you include in your manifest?
2. If you had cabins marked GUARANTEE on the final manifest received from a Tour Operator, what steps would you take to get finality on a cabin number before you depart? Who would you call and how might that scenario play out?
3. How would you handle Confidential Client forms?
4. How would you decorate a door sign? Use your logo to promote?
5. What would you suggest including in your own welcome letter?
6. What fun gift ideas can you bring to the cruise?

CHAPTER 4

EMBARKATION

༄

Preparation complete and paperwork in hand, the big day has arrived. My flight to San Diego is beautifully decorated with bright sunny skies and cotton-candy clouds. I am excited to meet my new group and ready my new office at sea.

CLMPeace Travel has already sent out my Welcome Letter. (That's a good thing. I won't have to deliver it on the first night at sea but **you** can see it at www.CarolLeeMiles.com – Book/ Forms.)

While claiming my bags in the airport, I look around for anyone who might recognize me by my photo on the Welcome Letter but that doesn't happen. I don't have a transfer voucher (meaning I would go on a bus provided by the cruise line), so I grab a cab and you guessed it — keep my receipt.

KEY CARD/CASH-FREE CRUISING

Cruise ships operate on a cash-free system. Key cards (similar to a credit card) are used when purchases are made and to record passengers going on and off the ship. All charges are automatically put on individual accounts and settled at the end of the cruise.

I know time is of the essence as embarkation day is always filled with lots of things to do so I'm happy to get checked in and receive my personalized key card. I learn the cabins are ready and it's off to work I go. Yes, it always makes me excited to board the ship, even though I might have been on the same one before.

When cabins are ready for check-in early (or at least early boarding on the ship is allowed for all passengers), the time factor is a big benefit to the Cruise Host. Waiting around in the terminal seems to make time drag. I'm thrilled to be back near the water and rush off to explore my home and office away from home.

OK, so NOW comes the real excitement!

CABIN

The adrenalin starts pumping as I board the ship and find my cabin on the outside with a window. (Outside cabins have a window, porthole or sliding door to a balcony. Inside cabins have no windows, are usually smaller in size and seem rather confining as it's impossible to check the weather before dressing for the day.) I'm happy it is outside this time – but believe me, I have experienced almost every type of cabin from a tiny inside (I lovingly call it a broom closet) to a balcony. Even when I am a bit disappointed with my cabin, I do *not* let that spoil my day.

Cabin changes are not made on Day 1 anyway, and now is my time to explore. My group will be looking for a smiling face. Smiles are both welcomed and embraced by our clients as well as ship staff.

Immediately I deposit moneys, jewelry, passports, etc., in the self code-operated safe in my cabin. (Most all ships have in-cabin safes in today's market. Occasionally I might need to utilize a safety deposit box at the Purser's Office, but not much anymore.)

I meet my Cabin Attendant Celina and tell her about the box I am expecting. Next I unload my hand luggage and peruse the ship's newsletter for today's activities, making a mental note of various times, locations and general information.

1. Time of mandatory lifeboat drill. (This is a ***must*** for everyone.)
2. Location of life jacket and muster station.
3. Location of food service upon boarding.
4. When and where the maitre d' can be found.
5. Location of Purser's Desk.
6. Spa, Casino and workout facilities.
7. Location of Shore Excursion Desk.

8. Location of Medical Facilities.
9. When ship staff will be introduced.

(These locations and times are simply a mental reminder as I have already checked out the ship by that magical tool called the Internet.)

I note the t.v. channel playing ship info, movie information, important announcements, demonstrations and general information. On most ships, including this one, I note the channel number so I can direct clients to this information source.

I sort my supplies and **carry with me** the following:

1. Small ship diagram left on my desk.
2. Copy of Embarkation Day program after briefly digesting the day's activities.
3. Copies of my group manifest and business cards.
4. Note cards in case I miss someone from whom I need answers.
5. Contracts for parties and shipboard credit or delivery arrangements.
6. Markers for a flip chart at my hospitality desk.
7. Notebook and Desk Hours stand for desk.

SHIP FAMILIARIZATION

If you are not familiar with the ship, this is your opportunity to get your exercise for the day. The good part about the Internet is I have already gone online to "tour the ship," but I am such a visual person it's great to see everything now first-hand. Usually even numbered cabins are on one side of the ship and odd numbered on the opposite side.

As anyone who has been on a cruise knows, ships can be confusing! But once you get the layout firmly in mind, everything will fall into place. Between each major bank of cabins on every deck, there is a schematic of the ship on the wall near the elevators. A map, basically. I use this resource personally and for others quite frequently.

If I am stopped and cannot answer a question as to a particular location, I take the person asking over to the ship diagram and point to where they want to go as well as tell them which deck to get off on. I use this resource often throughout the cruise.

There is always a welcome buffet, usually found on the LIDO deck, and I grab a quick bite as I prepare to roam. It might be awhile until dinner, and we hard-core cruisers never want to miss a meal on a cruise ship.

The following are areas I mentally take note of as a quick "buzz around the ship" helps me get my bearings:

1. **Dining rooms.**

    The Maitre d' is stationed in an area around the main dining room. He is not busy when I pass by, so I take this opportunity to stop and introduce myself.

    Some in the group have special dining needs and/or celebrations during the cruise so I leave him a manifest and point out those notations.

    The Maitre d' has just had 2 couples change from early to late fixed seating (probably Europeans, as they tend to eat later) so I quickly get my 2 couples that are wait-listed for early seating changed. They will be happy when I give them the news so I make a note to call them and let them know.
2. **Main showroom.**
3. **Promenade deck** – Often where shops are located and good for walking all the way around the ship on the outside deck.
4. **Medical facilities.**
5. **Movie theater (if there is one). Note**: Some ships now have movies on an open deck as well as an inside location for inclement weather.
6. **Cocktail lounges, casino, disco, children's area(s).**
7. **Spa, gym, beauty salon, pool(s), hot tubs.** (Pick up 1st day promo(s).
8. **Internet café.** (Pick up 1st day promo(s).
9. **Casual coffee shop; library.** Note if charges apply for specialty coffees.
10. **Soda Cards.** Note if special charges/savings apply.
11. **Smoking area if one is assigned inside.** (Sometimes there is a cigar bar.)
12. **Specialty restaurant(s) and charges for each.**

Ask how charges are handled and how tips are paid. (Often the client can charge the meal(s) to his/her account, but tipping is done in cash at a Specialty Restaurant.)

INTRODUCTION TO SHIP STAFF

Purser/Front Desk/Passenger Service

The purser's office (may be called by other names) is generally known as the "financial heartbeat" of the ship as well as an informational source for about any subject.

All finances run through this location – including credit card records and cabin reconciliations on a per passenger basis. Sometimes it is possible to buy stamps here, mail letters and even exchange money for foreign currency if it is available.

This office is an important **Cruise Host resource** for many pertinent details – and should rank at top priority status when getting on any ship. This cruise is no exception, so I pull out my "check-list" to make sure I cover all the questions I have.

PURSER OFFICE CHECK-LIST

1. **Be polite and courteous.**
   This is my first impression with a staff that is invaluable to the position with the group. I put on my warmest and most heart-felt smile while introducing myself with confidence and gratitude for their services, knowing the first day of any cruise is extremely long and hard for their staff.
   Everything is new to those getting onboard, and often tempers are short following travel uncertainties and questions are numerous. Mentally I say 'be patient' as I interact.
2. **Compare manifest with ship computer records.**
   Make certain cabin occupant's names and cabin numbers are in agreement. (This may take some time, but after all you are confirming information for a number of cabins. This keeps all those individuals from having to come to the desk.) While in the records, check to see if **shipboard credit** has been applied.

3. **Confirm GUARANTEES.**
   Get an actual cabin number for GUARANTEES if those assignments are not available when leaving for the cruise.
4. **Leave a manifest and business card.**
   Make sure my Name and Cabin number are clearly marked on both. Politely ask if I can be notified if an emergency comes up with one of my group.
5. **Find out the Staff member's name, title and office location** for the person who will handle the group's parties.
6. **Ask about Hospitality Desk location.**
   Ask who is in charge of arranging for the desk and double check the location if printed information has gone out to clients.
7. **Advise them if boxes of gifts are being delivered to the ship.**
   Leave information as to how many boxes are expected and by what means they are to arrive.
8. **Ask about seasick medicine.**
   Medicine is available in the gift shop or at the medical facility onboard.
9. **Captain's Welcome Party.**
   Ask when first party will be held.
10. **Door Decorations.**
    It is okay to place on cabin doors.
11. **Thank You.**
    Always leave with a sincere "Thank You."

Note: Sometimes a "Group Coordinator" or "Passenger Services Representative" is assigned on the ship, and this staff member may work directly with you for your group arrangements plus be able to answer many of your questions.

If this is the case, the Purser's Desk (or other term used by a particular cruise line) still remains the "Business Center" for all account and/or money-related matters and leaving a copy of the manifest with BOTH departments is appropriate to keep all bases covered.

FOOD & BEVERAGE OR BAR MANAGER

The Bar Manager is usually the "ace in the hole" for successful parties and/or planned events. What do you think? Does it benefit your group for Bar Manager Jorge to see you as a professional? Absolutely! If you work through a Group Coordinator or Passenger Services Representative, the same is true.

CHECK-LIST FOR F&B OR BAR MANAGER

1. **Confirm dates, times, location of events.**
   If pre-booked space is assigned, check out the space and see if it will work well for the group. If there is no pre-booked space, get group space secured now if at all possible. If not familiar with the ship, ask the Bar Manager (or other ship personnel handling your group) what space they recommend. Agree and then go check it out.
   If another space might work better, go back and see if the space can be changed. Remember – do not demand. Ask politely as any professional would do.
2. **Confirm microphone or other services needed.**
3. **Confirm party invitation arrangements.**
   Note: Ships usually offer their card stock and invitations but there may be a charge for both cards and delivery. Know your budget and be clear about arrangements.
4. **Confirm what type food and drink will be served**.
5. **Confirm Captain's Cocktail Parties – Dates, Times.**

HOTEL ACCOMMODATIONS MANAGER

The Hotel Manager is responsible for cabin conditions and cabin attendants. If members of the group are to receive gifts during the cruise, the cabin attendants will probably have a role in the delivery.

In this case the Purser's Office will assist in deliveries, but sometimes the Hotel Manager assists in delivery arrangements. Be sure and carry a little extra money for tipping when cabin attendants make the deliveries. This builds rapport as they are recognized for their extra service.

If a particular cabin assigned to the group has a mechanical malfunction, the Hotel Manager may be able to help with correcting the problem or making arrangements for another cabin. Having a good relationship might bring about a cabin upgrade if there is one available.

Always be thinking "what is best for my client and how can that be achieved?" while onboard. The more staff connections, the more likely a resolution can be found concerning a problem.

SHORE EXCURSION MANAGER

I am not able to talk with the Shore-Ex manager today but will do so tomorrow as we have a day at sea. I leave a manifest and card with one of the assistants and briefly discuss our group shore excursion in Mazatlan.

A friendly hello makes the manager or assistant aware of the group. Sometimes you may find Cruise Hosts accompany some shore excursions in return for making notes about a particular trip or because the department is short staffed. Never **assume** you will be handed a free trip or expect priority treatment. As a professional, courtesy and kindness go a lot farther.

MAITRE D'/DINING ONBOARD

Though many cruisers are now enjoying "anytime" or "open seating" dining, clients may still choose "fixed" seating. Keep in mind some ships only offer "anytime/open" dining, some only "fixed" seating dining and some a combination of both. Again, know the dining choices prior to departure.

"Anytime or Open Seating" dining – Guests can eat anytime during certain hours in certain locations. This type dinner location may or may not require reservations.

"Fixed" dining – Guests eat at the same table and at the same time every evening in the dining room. An earlier time and a later time is designated.

As I was able to catch the Maitre d' early on, we got most of the group issues settled. I know from the Manifest Mr. and Mrs. Stears are celebrating a 50th anniversary and are signed up for "anytime dining." I will get back to the Maitre d' when I have more details about their celebration. As this is a special group AND it's a 50th, I want to make sure they are recognized.

Perhaps they will dine in the Pinnacle Grill, a specialty restaurant onboard the *Oosterdam,* for their celebration. The Maitre d' can usually help with that situation or check with the person in charge of making reservations for that place of dining. I also make a mental note again of checking on payment and tipping policies in the Pinnacle Grill as others may also dine there.

On the many different cruise ships in the marketplace, dining options are varied to say the least. Specialty restaurants have made a big "splash" in the cruise world of today. Again, know your product.

Some specialty restaurants are very expensive while others are very reasonable or even free. Obviously clients in groups have varied opinions about how they will dine while onboard. The travel budget is yet another parameter to keep in mind.

Cruise lines have become very innovative about how to provide the evening meal without having to stand in line with a tray or eat in one dining room every evening. Be sure you understand how the various choices are handled on the ship you are on.

Also be aware that reservations may need to be made each day for some types of dining while other dining areas may be open and clients are able to walk right in and be seated any time there is an open table.

If reservations are necessary in any of the various types of dining options onboard, it is helpful for you to provide such information to the group early on. For questions such as this, I am prepared with answers as I walk into the Welcome Party the second day onboard.

SPA MANAGER

If he/she is available, talk with the manager on the first day. Sometimes the Spa Manager will give your group a discount off a total spa package if enough sign up. Since it is pretty common for discounts to apply on the first day, you really shine in your client's eyes if you get an **additional** amount off the total package. The Spa is a big deal to many of your clients. Be aware of the specials.

INTERNET CAFÉ MANAGER

Again, if it is possible try and talk to the Manager about specials that are offered. The group will be very happy if you tell them about special deals before they become aware of them. You can never get "too many good deals" for your clients, and cruisers today do stay in touch with their everyday lives on the Internet even though it can be expensive onboard.

SPECIAL CLASSES/SIGN-UP

On some cruise lines educational classes are free; on others there is a charge. Sometimes there is a combination of both – so it can be very confusing. If there is not sufficient information on how classes are handled along with detailed pricing structure prior to boarding, get details before the first group function. This is very important because some classes tend to fill right away.

Being able to take special classes onboard is a big treat to some, while others don't want to think while on vacation. For those that do want to participate, detail is the name of the game. Some may assume they will simply walk in, sit down and learn while others may not be aware classes are offered. If space is limited, some may be very disappointed if you haven't shared that information with them.

Announcements can be made or you can use the flip chart for items such as this. Additionally when you make rounds to put Welcome Signs on cabin doors, you might inform them about specific items when you get a feel they may be interested.

CASINO STAFF

Oh yes. Let's not forget the gamblers! Even if it is a simple Slot Machine Tournament, these events can stir up quite a lot of enthusiasm for the group's interest.

Casinos are not open while a ship is in port. As soon as the ship gets out of port, however, the gamblers will be ready to take advantage of first-day offers. Also it is quite common for the ship to be at sea the day after embarkation. Knowing what "deals" are offered in the casino is welcome information to many cruisers. Be prepared with information about the casino (even if you have no intention of gambling).

Good cheer and obvious camaraderie can be built when members of the group become part of a cheering section for winners on the cruise. If it's Bingo or Casino, performing or winning pool games, FUN is always the name of the game to keep the group connected.

MEDICAL STAFF

Doctors and good medical staff are definite advantages in the cruise industry. Office hours for the medical facility are posted daily in the bulletin. Knowing the staff is very helpful in turbulent seas or if some crazy flu bug runs through the ship. Leave them a manifest though they may not call for privacy reasons.

Seasickness is common in rough seas and some clients will consult you about options. Though I don't recommend medical advice or hand out medicine of any kind, it is good to know where clients can go onboard for help if they need it. If it gets bad enough, the Doctor can administer a shot before dehydration becomes a factor.

It is also good to have had some exchange with them in the event one of the clients gets hurt during the cruise or if there is a sudden death. In either case, necessary hospital forms may become an issue. Hopefully that is not the case on our cruise, but I have had it happen before.

Occasionally a kidney dialysis patient may be in the group. Yes, even that is possible on some cruise lines with specific ships that cater to the dialysis service.

RELATIONSHIPS WITH SHIP STAFF

Good relations with Ship Staff are important for a variety of reasons. Some of the best information on ports visited comes from the crew. As the shops and casino onboard are closed when the ship is in port, the individuals who work in those areas are free to be out and about. If the ship has already been going to the ports of call, find out as much as possible the little "ins and outs" they have learned from exploring.

Another good source is the Shore Excursions Office personnel if you become friendly with them and they are not offended to learn all of your clients are not going to use the ship tours. This can be a touchy subject so you want to handle those relationships carefully.

For instance, ship personnel might know of an Internet café close to the dock where the group can catch up on home connections much cheaper than onboard the ship. Or they might have a favorite beach or place to shop or good place to eat off the beaten path.

They are most willing to share this kind of information if you have developed friendships along the way. These kinds of things make clients think you have traveled this way many times before, even if it is your first cruise to that region. Again, always be thinking of what you can do for your clients onboard to bring value to their over-all experience.

Now we are set to go as we've covered the basics. Are you ready for your first exciting Cruise Host assignment?

EXERCISES

1. How would an assignment with an inside cabin affect you?
2. What duties in your present job will apply to your cruise ship job?
3. Are medical issues a factor with you? Can you relate to the hospital staff or others staff members? How can these relationships make you more aware as a Cruise Host?
4. What would you do first when you board? Is that different from my written plan in this synopsis? How?

CHAPTER 5

SEA LEGS AND WELCOMES

When the ship starts moving, my 'sea legs' are set to go as I run up to see San Diego being left behind. A Holland America Bon Voyage party is in place with music, drinks, streamers and mariachi music. As I circulate around the crowd wearing my nametag, there is a group of women raising their glasses for a toast and turn to include me as well. (Hooray for the trusty nametag exposure.) It's my big group of ladies, toasting Beth on her retirement. They are joyful, showing me their new "bling blings" as I learn each gets a new ring every time they travel together. What a fun group! I sit and relax – putting some faces to names on the manifest – while feeling the smooth and inviting ripples on the ocean rock the ship ever-so–slightly. I'm in my 'happy place.'

It's always nice when there's a party atmosphere for leaving any port. After we share some laughs, I'm soon back to my Hospitality Desk posting messages. I know I'm now "working" – even my 'sea legs' agree!

HOSPITALITY DESK

It is usually not practical to have Desk Hours on Embarkation Day because there is too much time consumed running around and gathering information. If I see I will have time (depends on group size), I post on my flip chart at the Hospitality Desk I am available between early and late seating at the entrance to a particular dining room area, as I will be there anyway while waiting to go eat later. If time is short, however, I may not even eat in the dining room (which is the case tonight).

As soon as I have collected all pertinent information I need to communicate, I find my Hospitality Desk (usually located in a central are of the ship and assigned to me) and get it set up for the cruise. On the desk I leave a notebook where clients can write notes about being contacted (or leave it outside my cabin door if the desk is removed when I am not present). I also use a stationary sign that states when I will be holding desk hours.

I immediately start a flip-chart page with a welcome and information about the day's activities, sign-up locations and times as well as other pertinent information.

I post the day and time of the Welcome Party but do not give a location because I know it will be on their invitation being delivered to the cabin. (We don't want to invite the whole ship.)

Getting everything posted and being back in my cabin in time for the lifeboat drill is usually a feat in itself.

Either way, the lifeboat drill is a must for everyone. At this point I may or may not have met anyone from the group, yet I have been racing around to set up everything for them as comfortably as I possibly can.

I'm relieved when I arrive back at my cabin after my explorations, staff meetings and getting my Hospitality Desk set up. The box of gifts and my luggage are in the cabin. This is a huge relief. If it hadn't been there, of course, I would start a search beginning with my Cabin Attendant Celina, and going through the Purser's Office or Group Coordinator.

Usually the box(es) are onboard somewhere and eventually show up in my cabin. Sometimes I get a call to come and identify the boxes, and once the boxes came to my cabin opened with some gifts missing. Now that was an interesting scenario. Thank goodness I had extras!

Most probably, however, they arrive in a timely manner. Next is the matter of arranging them in the cabin so I can still walk around. If there are over 100 people in the group and I've been assigned to a smaller inside cabin with several gifts involved, it can get to be tricky. That's when I smile and use my creative talents for making the best of a tight situation. There's always the closet!

DOOR DECORATIONS/MEETING GROUP

I have some time before dinner to put some Welcome Signs on the doors. I know from my manifest I have two birthdays and elect to start with Mrs. Johnson's cabin. Placing balloons and a card on the door (hooray for curly ribbon), I start to knock as the door pops open with a friendly hello and a very surprised Donna Johnson. Our introductory conversation is full of excitement as we share our day's travel talk.

The Stears cabin is next door and they appear in the hallway after a walk and find the festive balloons, welcome signs and birthday talk. More introductions follow and I ask both parties to leave their Welcome Signs on the door throughout the cruise and tell them about tomorrow's day of parties.

Can you beat it? We're talking celebrations and parties on our first day together while others walk by, trying not to act curious but obviously impressed with all the interaction taking place. Those are the type cruisers that start asking questions about our group.

The cruise line normally places names of the guests outside their cabin door and that is a huge plus when making cabin rounds the first day/night. As I put up a Welcome Sign (on the back I write their name), I compare to the name the ship has. It's yet another way to make sure we are both on the same page.

When the door pops open unexpectedly and there they are, I can always glance at the name and call them by their given name when we first meet. I try and spend a little time with them so I can make some mental notes, plus I carry a manifest for written notes about the person or persons in the cabin.

I always try to get Welcome Signs on doors during the early or late evening on Embarkation Day. Even if I haven't seen all the cruisers, when they awaken they will know I have been there to welcome them after they retired for the night.

For our Mexico cruise I retire around 1:00 a.m. Yes, I'm exhausted, but also feeling very accomplished as I've met and talked with several in the group, attended the show so I now recognize various staff and all Welcome Signs are in place. A walk around the deck tops off my day as stars dance in the sky . Simply feeling the salty mist on my face while I stop to look at the swirling waters behind the ship lights my spirits and puts a spring in my step for tomorrow. There's a full moon tonight, and once again I stop to reflect on a day filled with excitement and wonder. That part never stops for me – put me on a cruise ship and I'll travel anywhere. Did I mention I love my job or that I get paid for this? I meant to!

EXERCISES

1. Do you ever use a flip chart in your present job?
2. Is it effective? Why?
3. Can you see how unexpectedly running into clients on the first day can initiate a bond with them?
4. Would a first-day late night bother you?
5. How do you see your personal energy levels affecting this job?
6. Does this first day onboard excite you? How?

CHAPTER 6

GROUP ACTIVITIES ONBOARD

∽

WELCOME PARTY

All right, let the party begin. Do you like to throw parties? I do, especially when my paperwork says the cruise line is paying the bill. Remember when we talked about GAP points? CLMPeace Travel arranged for our party through the cruise line by using some of the Group Amenity Points. Our party is all planned with details in place. It is much easier on clients if you do **not** schedule a Welcome Party on Embarkation Day. Clients are too busy finding their way around and may have travelled long distances to get to the port. Time change is also a factor and they want to unpack and get settled.

For our party the next morning I arrive at least 15-20 minutes ahead of the scheduled time to make sure chairs are arranged for conversation, I agree with staff on what food and drinks are to be served and make sure equipment is in place if needed.

I introduce myself to the bartender (Sam) and wait staff (Roger) that will serve our group. I make note of their names as they will be the recipients of my cash tips as well. If for some reason I don't get them paid today, I can always work through Jorge to get the tips to them later.

I ask Roger to carry drinks on a tray when the guests arrive and make an announcement when the majority arrives as to what is being served. Having the morning party such as we are doing helps hold costs down. "Fru-Fru" drinks can get out of hand. The system used above holds ordering specialty drinks to a minimum.

Tour Operators are always appreciative when costs are monitored closely.

Since we arranged for a morning party, the Bloody Marys, Mimosas and non-alcoholic fruit juices are flowing as I welcome each and every cruiser in our group. I look out over the aquamarine waters while we get to know each other in an informal and informative way. Does it get any better? My 'office location' has just changed again as I meet and greet the entire group.

The nametags clients received are a part of the party atmosphere as new friendships begin and the group as a whole connects. I love this part of my job. Isn't party hosting a good way to start your day?

We have 100% attendance and have a 100% successful morning at sea. Bridge players connect. Golfers connect. Gardeners connect. Photographers connect. Game players connect.

I give clients a number of ways they can make good use of their time by coming by my Hospitality Desk and allowing me to share information I have stored in my head from the last 25 years of travel. As I now have an understanding of the Shore Excursions offered, I can visit with them about those as well.

Now we have the chance to talk about our group Shore Excursion in Mazatlan with King David. Excited chatter about our group excursion runs high after I explain the details of the trip (and recognize CLMPeace Travel for including this "extra" for everyone.)

Since new friendships have been formed, I suggest we have a CLMPeace Travel team for "Name That Tune" in the piano bar before dinner and ask about interest in the Karaoke contest. In short, whatever activities lend themselves to group get-togethers onboard I definitely encourage. Enthusiasm about group participation is evident. It's a good group.

I tell them about a handout at the desk for quick and easy steps for great guacamole (since we are in Mexico) and a quiz for anyone who wants to enter. The prize for the first one at my Hospitality Desk this afternoon from 2-3 will be a cup of specialty coffee at the coffee bar (and I get to join the winner after desk hours tomorrow.) This is a good way to get to know individuals on the cruise.

Anything that keeps the group coming back to the desk and interacting is good. Inexpensive prizes are good. You don't have to break the bank to have a good time. My Tour Operators will usually spring for a little kind of "slush" fund to keep the clients happy. Remember the receipts go in that special envelope.

If you don't have the years of experience part of having traveled a lot, what you do have is the opportunity to tell them how you have information on all the ports we will visit. Again, know the product and know the ports of call. Research is so incredibly easy in this day and age. Turn on that computer and go for it.

If they come up with sources of information you haven't even thought about, be confident in telling the client thank you and record them for your next trip. It's all about the learning and making the next cruise experience even better. In short, make yourself invaluable to the clients' cruise experience. It's that simple. Sell yourself. You'll be glad you did. It makes dollars and ene!

Note: Though we've already covered some information for our Mexico Cruise under "Welcome Party," the last part of this chapter is more of a generic overview of ideas you can use on any cruise you are hosting.

POSSIBLE "FLOW" OF WELCOME PARTY

For the first meeting with the entire group it is important to be relaxed and friendly, yet confident all the same. Having done the homework, it is easy to be well versed on the ports of call. Having good information to share brings enthusiastic response from any group.

Not knowing the group, this is their *first impression*. Perhaps they have never had a Cruise Host before or perhaps they think they don't need one now. Some probably have not cruised before while others have cruised numerous times.

What is important is they go home with a desire to repeat another cruise together – and that includes traveling with a professional Cruise Host. "Make it fun with confidence" is a good motto.

1. **Welcome guests/Introductions.**
2. **Icebreaker Game** (if there is no interaction).
3. **Location of Hospitality Desk, Hours, Flip Chart.**

4. **Planned Group Activities and/or Group Tours.**
5. **Time/place for group photo if one is to be taken.**
6. **Classes onboard** – give details and sign-up requirements.
7. **Spa or Internet specials.**
8. **Tipping.** Explain the automatic per person per day charge on the bill.
9. **Extra Charges.** For instance, specialty coffee or in some cases special ice cream treats.
10. **Soda/Wine Programs.** A soda card or special wine program is sometimes available if clients drink enough of those types of drinks throughout the cruise they want to participate for extra savings. Know the programs.
11. **Cabin.** I always give my cabin number out at parties, but never post it on a flip chart for public display.
12. **Other Gathering Places.** Suggest a drink bar for sing-a-long, and some different areas for dancers, making it clear it is a place to meet but drinks are at their own expense.
13. **Thank You.** Thank staff (Sam and Roger). Also thank the cruisers for sharing this special time.

OTHER GROUP ACTIVITIES/INFO ONBOARD

Here is a list of *some* possible events available, though activities vary a great deal from cruise line to cruise line:

1. BINGO! Bingo is big on cruise ships. Stay up on the group winners. Everyone loves to hear about a winner's good luck.
2. Slot tournaments, Blackjack – whatever the game, make the winners known.
3. Talent show. If group has participants, bring out the supporters! Stay INVOLVED.
4. Masquerade contest. It is funny to see what outfits can be devised from a simple garbage bag!
5. Best hat contest. Suggest meeting together to encourage other's creativity.

6. Pool contests. Have a person in the group who has "sexy legs" or plays pool volleyball? Get them to participate, and keep those rowdy group cheerleaders on the sideline.
7. How about Trivia? Late night bar laughs go hand in hand with a Trivia Contest or a favorite piano player onboard.
8. Dance contests. Go find a partner and show the group how winning the jitterbug contest in high school prepared you for Cruise Hosting – and "Dancing With the Stars" may be next!

Groups love to see a Cruise Host participate in the activities onboard. Stay involved while enjoying cruise time at sea. Clients will enjoy their time right along with their special Cruise Host.

REPEAT PASSENGERS' PARTIES

Cruisers quickly become attached to a name brand cruise line because repeat trips offer them some advantages. A "repeater party" is normally hosted by the Cruise Director with the Captain there to welcome everyone and give special recognition awards for repeat travelers.

Some in the group may be invited to these special parties while those who have not cruised with the line before are always intrigued as to what goes on. They are a good topic of discussion between group members and stimulate conversation and interaction about cruising more.

At the parties free drinks are usually served as well as hors d' hourves. On some ships a luncheon might be held in honor of repeat passengers. With so much competition in the cruise world today, special attention of this kind is commonplace.

PORT INFORMATION

It's not necessary to go OVERBOARD on this. The ship gives extensive port information during the cruise, including maps and places to shop. To duplicate the information is a waste of time and materials.

Ships generally have a port shopping talk where someone from the cruise line talks about reputable places to shop while in port. This is a cooperative effort between certain shops on land and the cruise line. These shops guarantee their products for quality, returns, etc., and are generally known to stand behind their guarantees. I've had occasion to know this works.

Some cruise lines have a staff member, author or other resource person such as a Travel Guide give talks on the port stop itself such as culture and history as well as what to see and do. This is a concept brought about by popular demand. Many cruisers are not interested in the shopping, but are interested in the history of an area. Others could care less and want to do their own thing. This is the good part about cruising. There is something for everyone. I've already met and talked with Dani Moore, the Travel Guide on our cruise. She's dynamite!

If you want to give out pertinent information on a particular **topic** when visiting a certain area, provide a handout pertaining to related subject matter. You can use those for getting clients to the desk or use them for a group get-together – even a handout under the cabin door with logo keeps them aware you are providing something special. Like the recipe I brought along for guacamole, stay with a destination kind of 'theme' when you prepare. I've even made a special "salmon" cookbook for Alaska cruisers. It all depends on budget of course, yours or the Tour Operator's.

Extra information, though not necessary, provides the opportunity to put a "letterhead mark" on the handout, keeping the mental awareness of your agency or Tour Operator in front of the clients. Sometimes special briefings can be used for this purpose if a Tour Operator requires extra educational time together. Once again, it all depends on the Tour Operator or what you choose to do on your own.

Another idea is to make the subject matter more entertaining such as a cute poem on an Alaskan adventure about salmon swimming upstream, perhaps bringing in Alaska as the next cruise itinerary that is offered. Always keep them thinking about that next cruise with the company. It's a win/win deal.

A game or puzzle can be used to educate the client about the region where you are traveling. Use your own creative talents to educate – if that is the direction you choose to go. Bottom line is be relaxed and confident with what you choose to do.

As previously noted, participating in activities onboard is a great way to build camaraderie and enhance positive group dynamics. Laughing through the "legs contest" or winning a trivia round keeps the group in high-energy mode.

EXERCISES

1. Have you hosted parties before? Do you have a flair for such?
2. What other areas on the ship do you have experience in?
3. How can you incorporate your own life so far into the cruise experience?
4. Are you comfortable on stage or in the limelight? Why do you feel you are or are not? Can you become better?

CHAPTER 7

ADDITIONAL KEY STAFF ONBOARD

I will not attempt to name all the staff, but these are a few more with whom you will be in contact.

CAPTAIN: Master of the ship. You may or may not have direct contact with the Captain, but he is visible when hosting parties onboard. On most voyages he hosts a welcome and farewell party. Often pictures can be taken with him.

When I am introduced to him at one of the functions, I always introduce myself and share my Tour Operator name and how many we have onboard.

CRUISE DIRECTOR: Master of Ceremonies on the cruise. Considered the energetic pulse of the ship, the Cruise Director introduces many of the daytime activities as well as entertainment in the evening. He/She may also have an assistant recognized onboard.

FUTURE CRUISE CONSULTANT: An expert on what cruises are available through the line. Takes deposits for future cruises, usually a set amount for the client's next cruise with the same cruise line and sometimes offers other benefits to booking while onboard.

Note: The booking automatically goes back to the Travel Agency who booked the clients on the present cruise. It is good to advise clients how this is handled.

MEMBERSHIP CONSULTANT: Has past records of clients' cruises with the same cruise line on which they are traveling. Handles questions regarding status and ranking. How clients are categorized or ranked when traveling numerous times on the same cruise line is very important because of increased benefits with each new level attained.

EVENT/ACTIVITIES STAFF: In charge of activities onboard, including children's programs. You will find lots of energy in these staff members as they try and keep cruisers involved and enjoying themselves.

TRAVEL GUIDE: Serves as a destination expert delivering multimedia presentations about the ship's itinerary (on some cruise lines). The Guide is like a one-stop resource for guest's questions about the ports of call. If there is such a person on the cruise, the contact can be invaluable to the Cruise Host.

Note: If there is no Travel Guide as such, the person in charge of shopping tips can be helpful. Either or both (when onboard) are valuable sources of information.

ENTERTAINERS: Entertain passengers with cabaret acts and "Broadway style" stage shows.

CABIN ATTENDANT: Takes care of a set of cabins for the entire cruise with service at least twice a day. Also sometimes involved in Room Service delivery.

SOCIAL HOSTS (sometimes called Ambassador Hosts or Gentlemen Hosts): Unfortunately Social Hosts aren't used as much as they used to be. They do have a significant place on cruise lines, given the fact many cruisers are single women who like to dance. On some cruise lines, however, Social Hosts are still available – they dance with ladies and generally socialize in a professional way. They may help with Shore Excursions or dance lessons as most have professional ballroom dance experience. When onboard I invite them to parties, especially if I have several women in the group.

Note: If you are a Tour Operator and have a group of lady dancers who want to book a cruise together, look for the cruise lines that have the hosts. It's a good sales point to know about. There are certain types of cruises that are geared toward dance themes – keep that in mind with the dancers in your portfolio of cruisers. When you are hosting a group with several single ladies, it is perfectly acceptable for you to ask the Social Hosts to pay special attention to your group. They are happy to do so as good comments keep them invited to return.

COMMUNICATION WITH STAFF

Staff members often have notes left in your cabin with specifics about upcoming activities or meetings. In most cases you will have an extension to call when trying to contact them.

If it's not possible to make contact with the Bar Manager after boarding, for example, leave a manifest, business card and note attached about the group. Sometimes functions are booked ahead of time, but occasionally some details are not in sync. Double-check all arrangements with the person in charge.

A thank you note or small souvenir from your home state/country for the Bar Manager or other staff member who goes out of the way for the group is always received with sincere appreciation. Even a local post card purchased at one of the ports of call will do. Continue to establish those long-lasting relationships. It's fun going back on a ship and being greeted with a smiling face from a previous cruise.

EXERCISES

1. Do you interact well with people?
2. What type job associations in your present employment would aid you with key staff members on the ship?
3. Can you think of other staff members that might be important to your group? Why?

CHAPTER 8

SHORE EXCURSIONS

I'm excited to say there has been a lot of traffic at my Hospitality Desk since the Cocktail Party. I was able to share some great information about shopping in Cabo and several came back to report their finds.

Those who aren't doing shore excursions typically drop by the desk to get some "inside scoop" on the next port, while others who are booked on shore excursions often want information to fill up those last two hours in port so they can get the most for their time allotted. They are pleased with their purchases and have enjoyed the little hole-in-the wall places I recommended for their special margaritas, too.

KING DAVID GROUP TOUR/MAZATLAN

So now comes the big Mazatlan day of exploring. Excited chatter fills our meeting place and we go off together to find King David's tour bus waiting for our group. His whole crew greets me with a friendly "Hola Carolina. We are happy to see you here again." (King David, as he is affectionately called, and his staff are well known in Mazatlan. David was crowned "King" by his staff when he was giving instructions one day and the title stuck with him.) They are always laughing and having fun – today is no exception as I am told "the King" will meet the group on the island.

We board the bus that takes us around to the smaller dock where I see Polo waving and waiting to be the Tour Guide on the smaller boat. I get another hug from my "Mazatlan family." The boat trip over to Stone Island is filled with informative "Spanglish" as Polo laughingly calls it. The group loves him and we laugh a lot during the scenic cruise. Groups always love the spontaneous information given and are quite surprised at what all they learn. The extravaganza is fun to watch.

After our welcome appetizer, served by other parts of King David's family, we climb on the 'island limo' ride that consists of a tractor pulling a wagon to tour around the island. The weather is gloriously sunny with a gentle breeze blowing as we bounce along an uninhabited beach that is one of my most favorite places in the whole world. Everyone is joyously happy today and laughing along the way, enjoying even more new friendships than from our first party together.

As we approach the quaint ocean-side restaurant where we will spend time and have lunch, King David appears in a tall 'Chef' hat and apron, just waiting to do his new demonstration on making salsa. We laugh and giggle, sharing his wonderful sense of humor while he entertains through his act in his own professional manner.

You wonder why I love my job? Who wouldn't? I meet the nicest people and get to hang out with many interesting friends from one corner of the earth to the other.

Hey! Here comes Miguel, wearing his typical cowboy hat and genuine smile, leading his horses for people to ride along the beach in search of sand dollars. This is just a small place of what I consider one of my heavens on earth.

After a typical Mazatlan-style lunch by the sea, the familiar pelicans accompany us en route back, making their dips and dives in the air for added entertainment. It looks as though they have been waiting to be fed as we return to the dock.

Cameras snap photo after photo and we get back onboard filled with even more chatter about the day. And just think, tomorrow we will be in Puerto Vallarta for a whole different adventure. Maybe we won't all be together touring, but I continue to share a wealth of information about activities there as well.

One of the best parts of being a Cruise Host is waking up someplace different every day, even if it's simply riding the waves and spending a day at sea. Hospitality desk hours are filled with stories from clients and ideas for their next adventure on land. Again, it's a win/win deal between all of us.

When traveling in places such as this where one can share "family members," such as King David and his crew, or sometimes simply looking toward new horizons and making new friends, it is always an exciting adventure – unpack only once to see it all.

OTHER SHORE EXCURSIONS

Reactions vary when the group of adventurers return from other shore excursions in Puerto Vallarta, the last stop on the cruise. The cliff divers are always a talked-about thrill in PV.

Some have enjoyed their own tours by taxi and some have taken ship excursions. Others have been quite content to drink margaritas and shop, the same as they did in Cabo. Life in the ports we visit is pretty laid back and so are the clients. This is a good thing in today's busy world. If I can continue to give them more value for their vacation, they will keep coming back.

EXERCISES

1. Have you traveled before and enjoyed shore-excursion type trips? If so, where?
2. With your experience in travel, can you bring to the table ideas for future trips together?
3. What about a walking tour in port? Does that interest you? Why? Would you be comfortable as a guide?

CHAPTER 9

ACCIDENT OR DEATH OF A CLIENT

∽

ACCIDENT

I am not immediately aware Mrs. Walker has fallen while boarding the ship after our Puerto Vallarta stop. Returning from shore and checking the message book on the Hospitality Desk, I find a note from Dr. Walker stating she has been injured and asking me to call their cabin.

Back in my own cabin the blinking red light on my phone somehow forewarns a distress signal, too. Calling the Walker cabin, I learn they are both there and tell them I will be up right away.

Quickly checking my manifest and seeing the Walkers have taken the ship insurance, I grab a copy of the Accident/Death report and take off up the stairs to their cabin. They are both smiling as the door opens and I see Mrs. Walker on the bed with her foot propped up, sporting an ice pack around her left ankle.

"Oh I'm so clumsy." she exclaims, "My foot slipped off that little bridge thing you walk up to board the ship because I wasn't holding onto the railing. I just sprained my ankle according to the ship doctor. It will be just fine, dear. My husband is a veterinarian and he thinks so, too. I'm sure it will be fine."

I am relieved to see the accident could have been much worse, yet feel sorry she has to suffer even at the very end of the cruise. My sympathies are quite appropriate and well received. Dr. Walker and she are in good spirits, too, so I take a report for the Tour Operator and suggest they may want to order room service for tonight and rest a bit. They agree.

Breathing a sigh of relief, I head for the Purser's Office and learn the accident report has been taken care of by ship staff and how quickly and comfortably the medical center onboard took care of her.

After thanking them for their help, I go to the doctor's office and thank the medical staff as well. They chuckle as they tell me Mrs. Walker arrived saying it was all her fault. We have been fortunate on this trip as this was the only injury and it was not a major one.

I return to the Hospitality Desk until the ship is ready to leave. Following desk hours, the sunny deck calls my name as one last look at Puerto Vallarta is recorded in memory. I smile and wave until the next visit – as I contemplate what could have been.

DEATH OF A CLIENT

Certainly death is something we are not anxious to deal with; however, a checklist is important when dealing with circumstances such as this. Everyone is a bit off guard, including you as the Cruise Host. The following are some considerations.

Believe it or not, at least one death often occurs on a cruise. Providing emotional support to those traveling with the deceased and helping the ship's staff as much as possible are both very important for the professional Cruise Host.

The way things are handled depends on whether the death occurs on the ship or while on shore in port. If the death occurs in port, the port agents will be involved in explaining whatever local laws and customs regulations apply and making arrangements for the body. The port agent will also handle all of the local reports required.

If ship staff reaches you either onboard or on shore, you can be a tremendous help to them. Remember it is the Captain's job to keep the cruise on schedule. Anything you can do to facilitate that will help.

Additionally, you will be a great asset to your group in putting their minds at ease. Some may want to talk about it; others may not. Either way, the Cruise Host is the professional, helping out in any way possible.

The following check list may be helpful. Note these are not set in stone. You may want to add more points – these are simply suggested guidelines for consideration, given the particular circumstances.

CHECKLIST FOR DEATH

1. **Never assume the client is dead.** Only a doctor can pronounce a person dead. If death occurs onboard, it is the doctor who fills out necessary papers and prepares the body.
2. **Get a statement of death**, including date, time and circumstances.
3. **Document passport** number, name on passport, birthday, date of issue, date of expiration, place of issue. If possible, take a copy.
4. **Get several copies of the death certificate** if possible.
5. **Notify your Tour Operator's 24-hr. emergency system** (if you are working for another company).
6. **Talk to ship staff about handling of the body:**
   A. **Disposition of the body; cremation?** Will body remain onboard or be shipped back from port? How will that be handled? If onboard, where will the body be stored?
   B. **Is a consulate involved?** (This depends on where ship is located at time of death.)
   C. **Who will notify next of kin? Should I?**
   D. **Who will notify insurance company?**
   E. **How will belongings be handled?** (It may be necessary to make a list, witnessed by ship staff – especially important if it is a roommate situation rather than a spouse.) Keep a copy.
   F. **Statement of death and receipt for the body.** (Do these documents need to be mailed, e-mailed or faxed home?
   G. **Can I help the medical staff in any way?**
7. **Focus on the deceased companion/spouse.** Write everything down as they will be in shock. For example, your phone # or cabin #, where you will be the next morning at a certain time, etc.
8. **Encourage them to call you often.** You also check in with them often.
9. **Remain calm and reassuring.** Your composure is key to the rest of the group feeling comfortable that everything has been done as efficiently as possible.

10. **Follow-up with your Tour Operator AND the family of the deceased**. You will be a big comfort to the family, being an integral part of the information gathered regarding the death.
11. **Be discrete.** Some will not want others to know.
12. **Have a group meeting if it is necessary.** An accident or death affects group members differently. Some may even consider leaving the cruise because of being upset by the whole situation. Be aware.
13. **KEEP A COPY OF EVERYTHING.**

DISPOSITION OF THE BODY

Decisions about disposition of the body are obviously made with consideration for international and local laws, and position of the ship at sea when the death occurred. It would be impossible to list every possible outcome.

Cruise lines deal with these circumstances routinely, and their staffs have the most up-to-date procedures. Your role is to be there for emotional support and hand holding while decisions are made within the guidelines of understanding.

If no family member is onboard, you may be working with the cruise line to locate the closest relative. Emergency contact numbers are recorded on the pre-boarding Passenger and/or Immigration Form through the cruise line. You might also refer to the client information sheets provided by your Tour Operator or you may have made up your own.

Be aware the ship may not be able to leave port until determination has been made about disposition of the body. Since there are so many parameters involved and circumstances vary, our role is to stand by and help in any way we can.

ADDITIONAL CONSIDERATIONS AFTER THE DEATH

The purser's office will need the deceased's passport in order to fill out the legal papers required by port agents and the cruise line.

Helping the bereaved by assisting with a simple task like finding the passport is monumental.

Probably the passport will be in the same location as the insurance papers if the deceased is insured. It will be necessary to collect all policy numbers, emergency contact numbers, etc., in order to alert the insurance company. Again, things like this are a tremendous help to the group member(s) involved and ship staff.

Helping make decisions regarding logistics of getting the body back home is another big item. It can be very costly to fly the body home. Talking through the options makes the bereaved feel like someone cares enough to help. Sometimes the loved one may fly on home while the body remains onboard until disembarkation at the home port. This is not uncommon.

It may be up to you to facilitate flight arrangements or help in making decisions.

If the spouse or traveling companion decides to leave the ship immediately, it is obvious that person may need help packing. If the survivor or companion wants to continue on the cruise, you can also talk with the Hotel Manager if he/she chooses to change cabins.

Being around to assist in making phone calls back home is another huge help to the one left. All of these considerations go a long way in a professional Cruise Host's over-all interaction with the cruise line as well as the group member(s) involved.

REMAINING GROUP MEMBERS

Usually group members experience anxiety when a serious accident or death occurs. It may be necessary for you to speak to the group collectively or on an individual basis to put minds as ease. Offer to do whatever is necessary in this regard.

You do not have to be a trained psychologist, but certainly hand holding during this time is well received. Sometimes group members feel uncertain if they want to go on with the trip even if they did not personally know the person involved. The whole incident is very unsettling, especially to older group members. Reassurance on your part is comforting.

It is amazing how often the companion of the deceased is the one who offers the most comfort. Sally may say something like "Sam would want us to go ahead and have a good time. Don't let this ruin your own holiday. We discussed this long ago."

ACCIDENT/DEATH REPORT

CLMPeace Travel has provided a form for an accident or death report in the paperwork I received prior to the cruise, however since she had insurance through the cruise line, they will complete necessary reports. In some cases, you might not have a form included so a generic one is provided online for your use. Feel free to change it to include other information you feel is necessary.

If you are doing your own, the form can be as simple or as detailed as you want. If the case is rather extensive, I would suggest you write a synopsis in your own words and attach a copy to the report.

See www.CarolLeeMiles.com – Book/Forms.

EXERCISES

1. Had you thought about the accident/death aspect of a Cruise Host job?
2. What experience can you bring along that would help you?
3. Can you add to the checklist I offered? If so, what?
4. Has anyone close to you had a medical experience while you were traveling with that person? How did you handle that?
5. Are you good at being that special shoulder to lean on in case of an emergency?
6. Do you have medical training? How would that help?
7. Can you think of other pertinent information that should be included on the accident/death report? What? Why?

CHAPTER 10

TIPPING POLICIES

On most cruise lines today, a per person/per day gratuity is included in the standardized cabin billing process and is reflected daily on the bill. The cruise line determines how the tip is divided.

For example a $10 pp/per day gratuity might be divided as follows: $4.00 to Cabin Attendant, $4.00 to Head Waiter and $2.00 to Assistant waiter or it might be even further apportioned to include other workers on the ship.

It is perfectly acceptable to ask how the charge is to be divided. It is also perfectly acceptable to ask the charge be taken off your bill and you personally hand the person whatever gratuity you feel is warranted. On almost every cruise clients will be confused about the tipping arrangement so be prepared to share correct information on the subject. Be informed by asking early on the details of distribution.

Keep in mind a good portion of the revenue collected by the wait staff and the cabin staff comes from gratuities. Many workers come from countries where employment is not available and anything they receive is appreciated. I always try and tip generously when they do a good job.

Every staff member on a cruise ship works hard but for some the physical labor is more intensive. Unless for some reason you have really poor service, in my personal opinion tipping is absolutely necessary. Of course if you want to reward someone for exceptional service above and beyond the person's call of duty, you can always tip that person more.

A good thing to remember is soft drinks, wine and alcoholic beverage charges have the gratuity built into the bill you sign when the drink is delivered, on most cruise lines. If you tip more, you are adding an additional amount to what has already been automatically calculated and is a part of the bill. This is a good "tip" for you clients. Also note that on some luxury cruise lines, drinks are included in the initial price paid so in that case you don't have to sign each individual drink ticket.

On the last day of the cruise some cruise lines will have envelopes for passengers to pick up in case they want to tip more to a particular individual. When this is done, a personal note is nice to accompany the rewarded effort.

Some cruise lines publicly state they have a "no tipping" policy throughout the cruise. I have never seen any staff person turn down the offer, however. The workers are usually just as tuned in to accepting tips as some cultures are to giving them. You will find various cultures vary their tipping according to their own standards. Discretion is left to the individual cruise passenger.

EXERCISES

1. What if someone tells you they refuse to tip? How would that conversation go between the two of you?
2. Would you have clients run a copy of their bill prior to the last day at sea? Why or why not?
3. Would you have difficulty talking about money to clients? Why?

CHAPTER 11

FAREWELL PARTY

Throwing a Farewell Party to say "thank you" is a good note on which to end any cruise. It also provides an opportunity to enhance the next trip you or your company is offering as well as provide a place for group exchange and goodbyes. I'm glad Mrs. Walker is going to feel like attending. She seems much better when we visit at breakfast.

As we've cruised the Mexican Riviera and I've gotten to know clients on a first-name basis, it will be fun to share some prizes for special talents I've recognized along the way. All this creates a friendly atmosphere for departure, and the gifts do not need to be expensive. Gag gifts are great, too, as I now know clients better and we can have a good laugh before departure.

Wrapped in curly ribbon, each of the prizes I award gives cause for smiles and applause. CLMPeace Travel has provided me with information about the next cruise itinerary (Alaska) so I am prepared with information about that trip.

Several clients have visited with the Future Cruise Representative who offered a future cruise booking with a $100 deposit. I inform guests their deposit will automatically go to the Tour Operator that booked this cruise (CLMPeace Travel) and I sincerely hope to be traveling with them again. I also ask if they have friends who might be interested in the same cruise as I continue to build business.

Additionally I have a farewell gift for everyone, the alarm clock. I have note cards printed from the Tour Operator with a special note (attached of course with curly ribbon!): "Set your alarm for our next adventure. It's time to enjoy Alaska. Sweet dreams, and thanks for cruising with CLMPeace Travel."

"FLOW" OF FINAL COCKTAIL PARTY

1. Thank everyone for coming.
2. Explanation of departure procedures.
3. Explanation of checkout procedures.
4. Encourage everyone to "wear your memories through a big SMILE." It's always fun to remember the good times shared on a cruise!
5. Prizes and/or gifts.
6. Brief information about the next group cruise.
7. A big THANK YOU is always appropriate to staff as well as members of the group.

PRE- OR POST-CRUISE PARTIES

Just think what a good time could be had by hosting a pre- or post-cruise party for the Mexican Riviera cruise if the group had been traveling from the same place and you are traveling with them. Margaritas and finger foods while kickin' up heels to some mariachi music would be ambiance plus. Simple decorations are cheap and easy. Set the stage.

Throw in some photos of past cruises and you have created a venue for questions and answers while talking about port stops and shore excursions.

Any documents or gifts such as the nametag at a pre-cruise party can be included in the fun. This also provides an opportunity to demonstrate how many different ways this simple "necklace" can be used. Be creative. Good marketing is a continual part of keeping good clients interested in cruising with you.

For the post-cruise party when a group has traveled all the way with you, perhaps you might open the invitation to friends of those who traveled with you to Mexico. Having already discussed the upcoming Alaska cruise onboard with other clients, the new friends may be ready to book after becoming a part of the good-natured atmosphere. In that case by all means have flyers and photos. A picture says a thousand words.

EXERCISES

1. How would you handle your Farewell Party?
2. Do you like doing extra little things for your friends/family? How would that play into the party scenario?
3. Can you think of other types of activities for a pre- or post-cruise party you would like to incorporate into your party-mind thinking?
4. OK, so you are planning your Farewell Party onboard.
    (a) Would you have it in the same location as the Welcome Party?
    (b) Would you serve the same type drinks?
    (c) What gift ideas do you have?
5. Let's switch gears a minute and consider this:

Let's say you are tired of this group of complainers. How would that affect your Farewell Party plans (or would it)?

CHAPTER 12

DISEMBARKATION

It's time to say "Goodbye" – but not with any sorrow because I am confident I have done my job well. At this point I have had many opportunities to talk with clients about traveling with me on another cruise and hopefully soon. It has been a great week at sea together.

During the cruise guests receive a form from the cruise line confirming their departure and/or flight time(s). Handling of departures is on a "timed" basis beginning with Independent travelers, followed by early to later flight times.

DISEMBARKATION TALK

A disembarkation talk is often held at the end of the cruise and this one is no exception. I suggest clients attend the talk as the disembarkation process will vary from cruise to cruise, ship to ship and port to port. My attendance is important as well plus I am available afterward for questions.

Often there are questions to answer as well as uncertainty on the part of your group, especially first-time cruisers. This talk is sometimes broadcast on television in case someone misses the general meeting, **or it may ONLY be televised.**

Every cruise line has a particular way of handling disembarkation, depending on country, port, etc. World situations also have a bearing. Immigration and Customs Officials will be responsible for checking all paperwork and clearing the ship before guests are allowed to get off.

Never give out information regarding disembarkation without first checking with staff about procedures. No matter how many cruises you take, the very one you are on right now may be the one with different rules and regulations.

LUGGAGE HANDLING
LUGGAGE OUT

Most cruise lines ask for passengers to place their checked luggage outside their cabin door between certain hours on the last evening of the cruise; ours is to be out by midnight.

This to-be-checked luggage will have a color-coded tag provided by the cruise line for easy identification once off the ship. Color-coding is dependant on specific departure information assigned earlier in the cruise. Clients will have different colors, dependant upon what arrangements they have made for departure when leaving the ship.

Hand carried luggage including toiletry articles for departure morning, medicines, passports & documents, change of clothes for journey home, etc., is left **inside** the cabin for departure morning.

Mandatory departure time from the cabin varies from cruise to cruise and is stated in the disembarkation information. Usually after breakfast, waiting in public areas until colors are called is standard procedure.

Express Baggage Services: In recent years, some airlines and cruise lines have started to provide cruise passengers a service sometimes referred to as Express or Signature Express (or other terms, depending on the cruise line).

This service may be available to some in your group and not to others. It is entirely dependant on the airline on which they are traveling and if that particular airline is a part of the service on that cruise. Some in my group are eligible for the Express service – while others are traveling home on an airline that does not provide it.

If the airline being used is a part of this service, clients are asked if they wish to pay a nominal per person charge, and receive their boarding pass for their flight before they leave the ship. The checked luggage is tagged especially for this service, and they most probably will not see it again until they reach the airport, either at the disembarkation city or at their home, depending on the rules of the cruise line and/or airline(s) being used.

Some in my group are confused about this because others have mentioned they are going to do it — yet their particular airline doesn't offer the Express service. If I haven't met up with those having questions yet, I will address it at my Hospitality Desk or at the Farewell Party.

Ms. Green is concerned some in the group are getting special treatment, so I assure her that is not the case. A brief explanation settles her questions and others as well.

Note this service is not found on all cruises, nor is it found with all airlines. It is necessary to ask at the Purser's Desk or carefully read through disembarkation material to see if this will apply to any members of your group. Guests with physical challenges or guests simply looking for more convenience often use this type service when they can.

The decision is theirs individually if they choose to pay the extra service charge for that convenience. Passengers who have used this arrangement in the past seem to agree it is worth the extra dollars spent. I have used it personally and agree wholeheartedly.

CONFIRMATION OF FLIGHTS

It varies from cruise to cruise and domestic versus international travel as to who confirms flights for the return home. As the Cruise Host, find out from the Purser's Office/Front Desk if they have capability for reconfirming flights and plan to do so — or if it is left up to you. I have been in both situations.

You may recall CLMPeace Travel requested I have an Internet account onboard. I work with the Walkers in confirming their flights and print boarding passes for them. The others seem to have taken care of it on their own, which is pretty common as most clients are 'Internet savvy' these days and feel more comfortable making their own arrangements.

FLIGHT ARRANGEMENTS

As the Cruise Host responsible for a group, you will probably be contacted by the Purser's Office/Front Desk to see if your group will be departing together or separately. If you are departing together, you will have the same luggage tag color and disembark at the same time, plus all clients will be confirmed on the same flight. In our case CLMPeace Travel clients have independent itineraries and will depart according to their own scheduled times. I inform ship staff of our arrangements when I receive the call.

Commonly there are two types of departure arrangements:

1. **Independent**: These guests make their own flight/departure arrangements. Additionally they will make their own arrangements for getting to/from the airport unless they have purchased transfers from the cruise line from ship to airport/hotel. Some may be getting off in the city where they reside; others may be meeting friends or driving somewhere else.

2. **Air/Sea**: These clients are generally booked through an agency or website, and use the cruise line's booking arrangements for both air and cruise. This includes transfers.

Note: Booking air/sea direct through the Cruise Line may cause some problems if clients do not understand they have little or no say in the airline booking procedure. Cruise lines often book flights according to the cheapest airfare; therefore, air schedules can be cumbersome with poor connections and long layovers.

CLMPeace Travel has booked flights for the entire group so there was better control over air schedules. This usually results in much happier clients.

Note: If clients are booking directly on the Tour Operator site OR booking their flights on their own through frequent flyer points for example, you might suggest they travel to the embarkation city one day early to be assured of boarding the ship in relaxed time. Airline delays can cause much stress when boarding a cruise ship.

Additionally when advising clients about booking their own flights home on disembarkation day, make sure they book their flight **after** noon to assure a more leisurely departure. No one can disembark until local authorities have cleared the entire ship, and this process can be rather time-consuming.

DISEMBARKATION PROCEDURES

Some cruise guests may prefer to handle their own luggage and depart the ship when called. Often these guests are called to disembark first, as the additional luggage in the passageways can be cumbersome.

This arrangement is made individually through the cruise line and a colored tag is appropriately assigned. Note this type departure can be very "unwieldy" as clients pulling and carrying luggage are sometimes mixed in with other departing guests in rather crowded spaces.

Most cruise lines color-code their baggage tags to facilitate claiming luggage in an orderly fashion once they are on land. Once the disembarkation procedures begin, the entire process takes little time. Guests are called to disembark according to their baggage tag color and proceed through the exit area and onto the dock where local cruise staff direct them to their luggage location.

If transfers to the airport are included in their departure arrangements, they will proceed to the coach as directed by cruise line personnel on the dock. Many on our manifest have made new friends and I watch as they team up to share taxis to the airport – a great idea.

Porters are available to assist both independent passengers as well as those taking transfers. Taxis and other shuttle services are available in the same area. Off they go.

EXERCISES

1. Do you understand Disembarkation procedures? If not, what do you do?
2. How would you handle it if a client insists he is not going to put his luggage in the hallway?
3. Do you think cruisers might get anxious about departure? Why? How would you handle this?

CHAPTER 13

PRE- OR POST-CRUISE EXTENSIONS

Sometimes a company will offer a pre- or post-cruise extension. This is not the case on our Mexican Riviera cruise. On this trip, my job began when I met the group onboard the ship and ended when the ship docked.

Had we had a **pre-cruise extension** (for example, Alaska is a popular destination for pre-cruise if the cruise is going North to South), I would have met my new group at the hotel where the land portion of the trip begins. After the land portion is complete, we would then board the ship together and travel home after the cruise is over.

In a similar Alaska example, if we had a **post-cruise extension** (ship going South to North) we would end the cruise followed by an included land package. The number of days of pre- or post-cruise varies according to the itinerary the client has selected.

In some cases there might be both pre- and post-cruise extensions. Usually any kind or kinds of extensions are offered to all clients, but it is left up to the traveler(s) whether they want to participate in the land portion(s) of the trip or not.

As plane rides and costly airfares sometimes have a bearing on the client's decision, some may choose to have a longer tour (doing land before and after) because of a physical endurance factor as well as the pocketbook expense.

In that case they might go early and tour, cruise in between, then stay afterward at a different location so they don't have to go back and repeat a long plane ride in order to explore the same region at a later date.

The number of clients who sign up for pre- or post-cruise tours may dictate whether or not the Cruise Host accompanies the group throughout the entire trip. That agreement is made between the Tour Operator and the Cruise Host.

EXERCISES

1. Do you think a pre- or post-cruise extension with the Cruise Host could have a positive effect on the whole trip How?
2. In our Alaska example, would you suggest your clients cruise before the land portion or do the opposite? Why?

CHAPTER 14

THE TRIP HOME

Our time together concludes on the ship with no post-cruise extension, so my last good-byes are at the Farewell Party or at breakfast the morning of departure when I see a few of the group. I always like to think in terms of "it's not the end, it's just the beginning of more and more relationships" with a company.

When I disembark to retrieve my luggage, I make a final sweep in the luggage area to see if there is that one in the group who needs special help. It only takes a minute to make sure they are in the hands of a porter or person representing the cruise line on land.

From that point on, I take a deep breath and know I have done everything in my power to make this cruise a favorable experience with and for my guests.

Next it is off to the airport with my luggage where I can now breathe a sigh of relief knowing they are all on their way home or to the next part of their journey. Some cruises seem like we just began and others seem more lengthy, depending on the group and the circumstances. It's the same with any job.

REPORTS AND FORMS – MORE PAPERS, PAPERS, PAPERS!
EXPENSE REPORTS

When traveling home alone, the airplane is a perfect place to make some notes and fill out some forms. Everything about the cruise is fresh and finalization is important in many respects.

As suggested earlier, expenses incurred have been documented and receipts kept in an orderly way. I review those to make sure they are clearly and properly marked with notes as to who or what the expense was for. CLMPeace Travel has provided a company expense form to be filled out which I review.

Note: It is helpful to make a copy of the expense form and have it with you on the return trip. Filling it out in pencil assures the final completion can be done quickly and concisely when arriving home and all expense records are complete – at least that works well for me.

If you are the Tour Operator, documented expenses and receipts are equally important for tax purposes. In this case you most likely have your own systematic way in which records are documented for an accountant.

At www.CarolLeeMiles.com – Book/Forms you will find an example of a generic expense report you might consider.

OVER-ALL RECAP

A general cruise report is always a good idea. The Tour Operator may or may not require a written report of this type, but you will find it a good record for yourself even if you do not send it anywhere.

You will want to make your own notes in whatever manner is most helpful for your records. Some points for consideration are as follows:

- The ship itself. What worked and what did not work as well. Note meeting space you liked for the size group you had or what you might want for a different size group.
- Dining Room and Specialty Restaurant service and requirements for reservations, cost, etc.
- Ship staff and logistics of working with a particular staff member, especially those responsible for parties.
- Shore Excursions. Price and value, coaches and guides used/ physical limitations.
- Cabin accommodations. Note specific problem-type areas to avoid as you find them.

- Designate other problem areas of the ship and make notes accordingly where you might want to change arrangements when you travel on the same ship in the future.
- Suggestions made by guests for improving your services or the logistics of the trip.

I enjoy writing this report this time as I replay in my mind various things that happened while onboard the ship and off. I'm hopeful I can travel with this group or similar types of clients again as we shared hearty laughter throughout the cruise. We also shared some heart-felt talks along the way.

THANK YOU NOTES

In general human beings like to get a personalized thank you note. CLMPeace Travel has provided me with extra note cards so I use extra airplane time to write some notes I will send off when I get home.

It was particularly enjoyable to take a variety of photos of various ones onboard, so I will include those after prints are made. The Stears' 50th was very special, and I'm glad to share photos to mark the occasion. My mind races to some of the "bling bling" photos taken for the "Beth's retirement group" as I smile. Every time they travel together, it's obvious the "Bling Bling Girls" have a blast. How fun is that?! And how fortunate am I?! My life is filled with abundance.

As I look out over the cotton-candy clouds and realize the Rocky Mountains are coming into view, I file away precious memories and drift off as I consider where my next cruise journey will take me.

EXERCISES

1. In your present job, are expense reports necessary?
2. Are you good at finalizing with good reporting methods?
3. How do you think your energy level will be after your Cruise Host experience?
4. Do you think you would want to repeat the job, knowing you will be experiencing new and different parts of the world?

5. Is Cruise Hosting a profession you think you would enjoy? Why or why not?

EXAM

1. Do you feel you passed or failed Cruise Hosting 101?
2. Did you learn anything new?
3. Did you feel connected to each step we took in the job experience?
4. How could/would you change various functions of the job itself to improve client relations?
5. Are you excited about Cruise Hosting?
6. Would you be interested in taking a training cruise to see if you like the job responsibilities and interaction with a group?

SUMMARY

Part I has taken you through the early stages of a cruise all the way through to the end. You have learned how to prepare for the cruise, what steps to take, what ship personnel are important to know when you board, ideas for making parties successful, execution of a relaxed shore excursion, what to do in case of accident or death, the process of disembarkation and follow-up after the cruise.

Of course, situations vary with every Cruise Host opportunity. No two groups are ever the same, nor will the participants react in the same way(s) to different itineraries.

Lots of things influence the success of a trip: cruise staff onboard, mechanical functions of the ship, weather-related conditions, food quality/quantity, activity or lack thereof, entertainment onboard, attitude of cabin and wait staff, officer interaction.... All these and more go into a person's over-all mindset as it relates to the total cruise experience.

Some groups you will love; others will be more difficult. Some will think you hung the moon while others can be less appreciative and more challenging. The beauty of it all is the Cruise Host becomes more and more efficient with every experience.

People often ask "Don't you get tired of travel?" My answer is: "I get tired, but I never tire of meeting new people, seeing new places and making new friends. When I feel I've added to a cruise group's experience and given them added value to their trip, I can go home saying to myself 'JOB WELL DONE.'

Who could ask for anything more?"

WHAT'S NEXT?

Career change impacts lives. Parts II, III, IV and V touch on ways in which people have taken charge of their own lives – including two case studies and my own story.

Fear of career change and the psychology of dealing with conflict provide food for thought in any given field. Let's now explore together as we embrace a future filled with profound abundance.

PHOTO GALLERY

GETTING PAID TO CRUISE

Ports of Call Days
Photos courtesy of Donna Johnson

PHOTO GALLERY 8

Ports of Call Boeing 707 Airplane
Photo courtesy of Richard Vandervord, UK
More airplane photos available: Richard@vandervord.plus.com

Proud Parents, Virginia and Walter Shannon
Virginia Shannon: Love Cruising with my daughter!
Photo courtesy of the author

PHOTO GALLERY

Kathryn (Kay) Shannon Bay, Shirley Shannon Thomas, CarolLee Shannon Miles, Virginia Burroughs Shannon With Mark Twain aka Riverlorian Lewis Hankins on A.Q. American Queen and Mississippi Queen
Photos courtesy of Shirley Thomas

Antarctica Aboard Society Expeditions
'Talking' with New Friends!
Photos courtesy of Margaret Rhea

Crystal Symphony Docked in Dover, England
Photo courtesy of the author

GETTING PAID TO CRUISE

Dead Sea 'Mud for the Wrinkles' Fun
Author re-baptized in the River Jordan
Photos courtesy of Janet Stears

On the Road to Jerusalem
Donna Hughes Johnson, Janet Stears, CarolLee Miles
Photo courtesy of Winola Uhrig

88 GETTING PAID TO CRUISE

A Camel Ride at the Pyramids
A Tiny Pyramid Rests at the Western Wall
Photos courtesy of the author

Proud Mothers on Mother's Day
Traci Miles Beauchene, CarolLee Shannon Miles,
Terri Miles Schmier
Photo courtesy of Michael Schmier

Holland America Line *Oosterdam*/ Mexican Riviera
Photo courtesy of the author

PHOTO GALLERY 91

ZamZuu Convention 2010, St. Louis, MO
YTB International, Inc.
1901 E. Edwardsville Road, Wood River, IL 62095
618-655-9520
Photo courtesy of PJ More

'King David' Perez Waits at the Dock
King David Company, Av. Camaron Sabalo #333
Centro Commercial Las Palmas L-8, Mazatlan, Sinaloa, MX
011 52 669 914 1444 www.KingDavid.com.mx
Photo Courtesy of the author

PHOTO GALLERY 93

Zip Line and Dolphin Fun
Photos courtesy of the author

Sapphire Princess Anchored at Cabo San Lucas, MX
Photo courtesy of the author

Back in the Days
Photos and Visits 'On the Bridge' were Commonplace
Photo courtesy of Donna Johnson

ITMI Symposium
International Tour Management Institute, Inc.
625 Market Street, Ste. 810, San Francisco, CA 94105
415-957-9489 www.itmisf.com
Photo courtesy of the author

PHOTO GALLERY 97

Aboard the Crystal Symphony in New York Harbor
Photo courtesy of the author

A Dove in Flight – Aboard Epirotiki in Greece
In the Studio – Recording Songs for 'Peace'
Photos courtesy of the author

PHOTO GALLERY 99

'Peace' CD
Photo courtesy of the author
www.CarolLeeMiles.com

100 GETTING PAID TO CRUISE

Abundance and Grace on the Oceans of the World
Photo courtesy of Larry Love

PHOTO GALLERY 101

Footprints Into the Unknown Future
Photo courtesy of the author

PART II

⁓

WANDERLUST MEANDERINGS

CHAPTER 1

SECRETS BEHIND THE BOOK

My adventurous and wanderlust spirit brought me to this page you are reading. As in, my story is not yet over. I could have published just a manual "Cruise Hosting 101," and it would have satisfied an audience of a certain kind. That would have been okay – but it would not have been the whole story. I'm an effervescent person, and I knew that some of the "secrets" of being successful (at this career, or others) also is dependent upon excitement. Adding more spontaneity, more craziness, more sensitivity made the book more real.

As I began to write, I considered how certain situations I have experienced might relate to persons in the travel field (or other fields) who are looking for jobs or who are considering a job change.

What I'm saying is: this book seemed to cry out for more depth and more meaning. It also seemed to want to reach out to more people. You may have picked up the book because you are a newly certified Tour Director and want to specialize in cruises – or perhaps you are an experienced one, looking for new ideas. Perhaps you represent a Tour Operator that is looking for new ways to keep clients happy, or you recently became a new Internet travel site owner and are looking for innovative ways to make the lucrative cruise part of your business a success.

There are many questions you might be asking yourself, big and small: Am I doing all I was put on this earth to do? Am I making a living in an exciting and engaging way? Am I attempting to direct my energy chakras into where the universe might be leading me? Am I wondering: Is this all there is to life?

And why **did** you pick up this book in the first place? Were you looking for a new career? Were you looking for a new purpose in life? Have you always wanted to go on a cruise and your appetite was whetted when you suddenly realized cruising could be a career? Do you represent a cruise line that wants to explore new avenues for working with groups onboard and you are eager to exchange ideas?

Perhaps the title of the book rearranged some neurons about cruising with your family and friends or even opened up some thought about income tax deductions. Whatever your own dynamic, I'm glad you're here and have an open mind to share some of my secrets.

Right now you have a chance to grab your bright orange life vest as together we jump into a lifeboat and row into our unknown futures.

EXERCISES

1. They say you can't judge a book by its cover. Is the person inside of you content with your outside appearance?
2. Are you using your own pen to write your own song? Why or why not?
3. Does jumping into the lifeboat excite you or scare you? Or a little of both?
4. How do you feel about getting out of your comfort zone?

CHAPTER 2

MY WANDERLUST CAREER

The term "wanderlust" describes me perfectly. Growing up on a farm in central Missouri, my favorite spot for exploring the unknown world was a big old maple tree in our back yard. It's hollowed and smoothed out bark made for the perfect embrace of my small frame and active mind as I mentally found a seat on a big silver plane streaking across the sky. Here, I could erase the sky, paint a deep blue sea in its place, and find my cabin on an imaginary cruise ship while my own mental meanderings carried me to various parts of the world. I spent hours embracing thoughts of my future.

Prior to my exposure to the real jet airplane world, my life-long experiences revolved around the safety net of home. As a child I sang at our tiny church near the farm and performed at little country schools in the area as a singer and dancer. Following a cheerleader role in high school I attended one year of college, became a young working wife, and then embraced motherhood. A little education was thrown in for dessert.

I'm sure you are familiar with the statement "Oh, I'm *just* a stay-at-home housewife and mother," and I myself used it to describe me. Don't get me wrong. I am proud of the fact I supported every move our family made to make a secure foundation for our two daughters who have grown into mature young women with families of their own. I'm proud of the part of me in them.

But I learned there is no such thing as being "*just* a housewife and mother." Living that role, however, my **MIND** had been wrapped around the "**just**" part for years.

I married at age 18 with one year of college under my belt, quit college to help educate my husband, raised two daughters plus two dogs and one cat, finally became a university graduate 20 years after high school (some of us are slow learners!) but never gave myself the credit I deserved.

At 43 years of age, I had never taken the luxury of knowing ME. Our youngest daughter, Terri, went off to join her sister Traci in college and I found myself roaming around this enormously empty home saying *"What in the world am I going to do when IIIIIIIIIII grow up?"*

EXERCISES

1. Looking back on your childhood, how would you describe yourself?
2. Have your dreams become reality?
3. Have you stopped to give yourself credit you deserve?
4. Do you describe your career as "**just**"?

CHAPTER 3

PORTS OF CALL TRAVEL CLUB

I explored several business options after obtaining my degree but nothing seemed to be right. Though my studies focused on the business world, I felt this strong desire to work in a field that lent itself more to psychology, and perhaps even entertainment of some sort. Always in the back of my mind was helping people in some way. Being in front of a crowd was exciting and fun as a child. Why not as an adult?

The answer finally came like a lightning flash when another educated 'housewife mother' suggested I apply for a job with Ports of Call Travel Club in Denver, CO. She shared some adventures about helping people in various parts of the world and I was intrigued. It just might fit. Or would it?

I felt childishly excited at the idea yet skeptical of how this would affect my home life as "flying all over the world" didn't seem to fit in my mental adult frame of mind. Our daughters were in college only 60 miles away, but Terri had just left the nest. What would happen if they needed me? And what about my traveling husband? How would that work out? A bit of fear about the whole process ensued. After all it would be a complete change of character role for me. Or would it?

After talking with yet another housewife and mother whose husband traveled a lot, several discussions followed with my family. As they supported my decision, I decided to try my wings and set out toward the adventure land I had always dreamed about.

When first applying for the job, I was turned down. By then my mental mindset was glued securely to the whole flight attendant uniform idea – so I refused to take no for an answer and started an all-out earnest effort to make my name known to Pam, the woman in charge of hiring. Additionally my friends kept putting in the good word.

Pam would answer the phone by saying "Yes, CarolLee, I know you want to come to work for us but the class is full and you were not selected," to which I would reply "OK, but I know I am supposed to be in that class." And then I would call back, time and again.

To my surprise **my** phone actually rang the day before the class was to begin in early 1986 and Pam told me another woman had dropped out. When she asked if I wanted to take her place, I started screaming. In my mind I was already in uniform as I quickly accepted before she changed her mind.

Being hired by Ports of Call Travel Club, affectionately known as POC, meant I would work as a Flight Attendant/Tour Director & Cruise Host with the unique great fortune of indeed flying around the world in 707 and 727 airplanes – as well as cruising on many of the major cruise lines. The company had been founded years prior by a pilot and his wife, Larry and Fredda Turrill, who all crews thank today for giving us this amazing opportunity for employment. Bingo! Wanderlust truly did find its place in my life.

Training was hard, but I loved the way our trainers attacked the whole learning experience with such professionalism. Standing tall in that uniform made me proud of this new person about to emerge.

We had our own check-in terminal where personal greetings by porters and ground staff started the day with big smiles. Members came early to socialize while waiting for a flight to depart. Passengers passed though the company's own security machine, then walked out to board the plane by climbing steps attached to a truck like you see in some smaller airports today.

Can you even begin to believe our taxiway was connected to the old Denver Stapleton Airport runway (which is now a shopping center) where we took off routinely? In today's world, post 9/11, such a procedure simply wouldn't happen. For a farm girl from Missouri, I found that uniform actually transformed me into a world traveler in nothing flat. I loved being a part of every intricate detail.

After training – which took several weeks – my first long assignment was 18 days in Ireland, Scotland and England. That trip was only the beginning of repeated and numerous international flights. The cockpit was never locked back then – we were all "just" family, exploring our tomorrows through space and time. My family world and my universe world expanded at the speed of light.

My feelings of "**just**" that housewife and mother exploded into glorious bursts of rainbow colors, colors that lit up the skies of education and experience. I began to see a very different world than the one I had always known and understood.

I became confident and a confidante. All of my years living in the "safety net of home" expanded into a real-life job out in the world of different cultures and customs. My work relationships and passenger relationships opened new doors of searching and understanding. I began to fly with new wings (literally!) as I became a new person, embracing every new destination with passion.

There were three crew in the cockpit, plus four Flight Attendants (FA's) on every 707 flight. As POC owned their own fleet of airplanes, the whole crew often stayed at the destination where the FA's took over as "tour directors." If we had no immediate duties with the group, the crew was off exploring in a rented van.

Groups were often large as POC membership was over 20,000. It was not uncommon to work a "Mystery Trip" where passengers signed up, paid X amount of dollars, climbed on several Ports of Call airplanes and had no idea where they were going until they landed. As an example of a Mystery Trip, we once handled nine coaches on Malta. Just think about that lesson in luggage control! In that scenario we (the flight crew) had staff from the Denver POC office plus a ground staff on Malta to help orchestrate the trip.

In quite another scenario, I was among the flight crew (turned Tour Director after landing) who handled passengers from two 707s parked nose to nose on the Grand Bahamas Island. On that trip I ended up with not one but several medical emergencies.

Keeping cool in the height of crisis became commonplace. Giving the passengers a sense of calm while preparing the cabin for an emergency landing or accompanying a family through a medical trauma was part of my new occupation.

CRUISING WITH PORTS OF CALL

With all the experiences I had on land, however, nothing could compare to cruising. Nothing could compare to walking on the deck of a cruise ship, feeling the mist of the ocean spraying over the railing. Nothing could compare to the exhilaration and absolute, ultimate feeling of "I have arrived. This world is mine. I am claiming this destination as my own."

Looking back on it, my first cruise was rather entertaining to say the least. Donna and I still chuckle about feeling like we should "back out in the hallway in order to put on pantyhose" because the cabin was so tiny.

How about brushing your teeth while your work buddy is using the "facil-i-twa" because the shower/sink/toilet are sort of rolled into one space with little room to turn around? Back up and your rear hit the bunk. Squeeze through and you are in the closet. Turn sideways and extend your arms up for the sweater because forward or backward you hit a wall. I don't think that ship even exists anymore. I can't imagine why. After all the 1980's seem back in dinosaur times anyway.

Even with those kinds of conditions I felt as though my connection with the oceans of the world was a mad passionate love affair that would never end. I simply knew I must somehow find a way to be on as many cruise ships as I could in the next phase of my life's journey.

I felt exhilarated. I felt giddy. I felt like life on earth had taken on new meaning. On that first cruise I felt as though I had written the first chapter for the rest of my life.

How could I cruise more? I had to make it happen, the question was how. How could I put all my personal efforts into a cruise ship headed into the unknown? What could I do to point the compass to every opportunity, every enriching experience, every "Love Boat" that set out to sea?

At POC we turned in a bid sheet monthly for various trips, which were explained in the magazine that went out to members describing details of the destinations offered. It would come as no surprise I always listed cruises first. More importantly, however, I visualized being on that ship, whatever ship that cruised with POC members onboard.

Eventually various clubs within the club were formed, so I volunteered to be co-chairman of the Cruise Club with a senior. She and I worked together to learn more about what cruises were out there and what we could suggest for new cruise experiences while we continued to educate ourselves on the various cruise lines. There was no Internet – magazines and books were our best companions in searching for new ideas.

The process was undeniably joyous. It was about that job no longer being a job or school no longer being school. It was all about **recess**. Having a ravenous appetite for adventure, what could I plan for my next play activity? What beaches of the world would I love to explore? The mental visualization penetrated my brain and filled my imaginary world that started to materialize month after month. The actual experience of being on cruise ships with groups fulfilled that childhood dream, and my world came to life in a whole new way.

MARGARET AND ANTARCTICA

A feisty little woman named Margaret was one of Ports of Call's favorite supporters, and she traveled often. She really didn't like cruises as much as land trips, but there were certain places she wanted to see so we happily became fast friends on several crystal clear oceans.

Margaret's sparkly eyes always lit up when she would tell me about who she had identified in her terms was the ATD (Alternate Tour Director – who always thought they knew more than I did). Her beautiful white hair sort of bounced in her springy and youthful step. She made a trip light up somehow, often with her good friends who had also traveled with POC for years.

When Margaret was in her 70's we were on an Alaska Inside Passage Cruise when she came to me with a frown and very stern expression, not typical of her character at all. In asking if I could possibly do something to help her, my response with a worried tone was "Of course, Margaret. I will try."

Then the devilment came out as she finally recaptured her normal grin and said she had never taken a white water raft trip – and would I consider going with her on a shore excursion. Of course my response was an exuberant "yes." Soon we were off on another adventure.

A favorite of my photos is the two of us in a rubber raft, secured in our life jackets with huge smiles on our faces as we are hanging onto the rope and riding the rapids.

Immediately after the trip was over, Margaret looked at me with her ever-present spirit engaged and said "How about Antarctica next?" I grinned as I hugged her and said "Sure. Why not!"

Perhaps, just perhaps, the stars in my travel universe were lining up as I started to envision Antarctica. I knew I could never pay for a trip for myself to Antarctica so I began to call on L-U-C-K. I **Loved** the idea **Until Creation Knocked.**

Sure enough, my senior partner co-chairman of the POC Cruise Club had been assigned the Antarctica trip when suddenly she was not able to go. I was assigned the cruise. Therein lies the "magic" of luck. I had positioned myself as a winner. I had used "The Secret" long before I heard there was such a concept to describe it, let alone a book or DVD.

The best part was Margaret and I would be traveling together again. One cruise experience built toward the next. From the appetizer of Alaska, the main course turned out to be Antarctica. In 1990, I stepped foot on my 7th continent, a mere four years after starting my travel career. I found my calling.

During those four years POC provided us with an additional training through the Denver Guide Academy. While we were in training, we realized we actually knew more than the teacher. Then another brainstorm occurred. Another bolt sent to my brain said "Oh, is there actually a better ***training*** for this Tour Director/Cruise Host field? If so I need to check it out."

When the creative mind is gestating, I've found sometimes all I need do is close my eyes and simply hang on for dear life. Before I had looked at the POC opportunity as more of a fun job, but could this actually ***be*** a career? Perhaps it was worth more investigation.

Was there something out there where I *could* learn more about the travel and tour industry? Hmmmm.

Obviously I was being presented with yet another nudge to find out more. My friends weren't interested in pursuing other options for one reason or another so I plunged into the open sea alone, rowing my own lifeboat where I found ITMI. You can read about it in Chapter 6.

EXERCISES

1. Does the thought of cruising excite you the way it did me?
2. Would you want to consider cruising in your long-term career goals?
3. Have you ever worked in a career that made you feel like you were at recess rather than working?
4. How happy are you right now, in your career?

CHAPTER 4

FINDING A PURPOSE IN MY LIFE

༄

Meanwhile, my "just" was replaced with a new title as I felt my mission had become spreading peace around the world. I unofficially named myself an "Ambassador of Peace" while traveling around the globe to places like China, Africa, Russia, Indonesia, Mexico, the Caribbean and Guatemala, to name a few.

Becoming an Ambassador of Peace, especially in third-world countries, opened new channels of thinking as international relations continued to be part of our every-day POC uniform. As I tried to feel another human being's role in an unjust living situation, I remembered words my Mom often spoke: you will always live your life trying to help other people.

She also said I would write and ironically enough, I did. When I explored my thoughts and deepest feelings through associations with other human beings, I began to search for answers. My thoughts always returned to the same question: What does the word peace mean to them?

And what does the word peace mean to me?

What is it like, that woman's Hell on earth, or does she describe it as Hell? What is it like living in a country like Guatemala, growing up in an indigenous society? Though I couldn't speak their village languages, I always felt a certain closeness to the women there – that sell their wall hangings for mere pennies compared to what they are worth. Do they have self worth? Often I counted my own blessings by comparison.

Visiting dung huts in Africa where flies flew around open sores and runny noses on children playing in villages touched my heart – and became an instant replay in my memory channels. Women and young girls having to walk long distances for water while continually afraid of being raped and beaten along the way, where is the justice in it all? I felt for every situation I was exposed to – deeply felt a certain connection hard to explain.

Touching and feeling the seemingly torn soul of a little old lady, wrinkled and worn from life in general, became paramount in my life's journey. That little old lady selling pencils, looking like she was 90 years of age while probably only 50, how many days in her life could she say she was living a life of peace? And what about the children?

What about the poor soul standing in line for milk while our tour group enjoyed meals accompanied by champagne and caviar? Visiting a home in Russia after the ruble lost all value and hearing a university professor state there is no work available and no hope for the future, where does one find a sense of peace and comfort in the muddle of Communism versus Democracy for example? And how does it all equate? I could only hug and hold that Russian woman, showing respect not only to a scholar, but also to another human being. As we embraced, I handed her the most personal gift I could give – a CD entitled 'Peace' – and told her she and her family would be in my prayers. As we wept together, we agreed: change hurts sometimes. And often it runs very deep indeed.

As I experienced these scenarios first hand, I did begin to write. It became too suffocating to keep everything inside. I had traveled the world and found myself light years away from my starting point. I finally felt respected in my own profession, yet also realized travel is indeed filled with longing and searching for answers. For me it all centered around the idea of peace: peace for all nations.

After I found writing, passion and abundance seemed to embrace my future – yet I still felt a strong desire to help make the world a better place in which to live. Writing to the sound of ocean waves illustrated more colorful rainbows as I began to dance to a song of peace myself, a subject that will be addressed later in the book.

EXERCISES

1. What experiences in your occupational journey stand out in your mind?
2. Is your career choice satisfying?
3. Are you looking for a new field?
4. Did you just graduate from some level of education? Are you looking for employment, full-time or part-time?
5. How would you steer your personal career lifeboat if there were no limitations?
6. Is your career field filled with abundance? How? If not, what would you change?

CHAPTER 5

THE END OF POC/ FINDING OTHER AVENUES

∽

Unfortunately, Ports of Call Travel Club did not last. Economics took over and the end of the club was near. On the horizon, however, there was hope.

I got a job and worked part-time in a brick and mortar travel agency. While learning more about the logistics of a travel agency, the experience of outside sales plus helping with corporate and incentive groups broadened my scope of the travel world in general.

Reference materials were bound or on VHS video (might be described today as the horse and buggy world of eye-catching opportunity), where I learned about such organizations as CLIA, Cruise Lines International Association and other travel organizations.

I continued the insatiable craving and building of information on the cruise industry while filing it away in my brain. Did I know why exactly? No. But I knew it was important. I knew *inside*. Rowing the lifeboat into my future enabled me to settle into a more peaceful place.

At that time things were changing in the way airlines worked with travel agents. Commissions were being reduced on airline bookings, and agency owners began looking for ways to increase income. The owner of the local agency had always been a good businesswoman, and continued "thinking outside the box" by concentrating more on group sales. Because of her foresight she kept her agents working when many other brick and mortar agencies did not survive. That continues today.

Expanding and building the incentive and corporate market also helped the agency compete in the marketplace. Working locally gave me some valuable experience, filled a space of time and provided an opportunity to continue learning how the travel and cruise worlds operate.

RELATIONSHIPS WITH BRICK AND MORTAR AGENCIES

Let me just say here that brick and mortar agencies have been instrumental in building the travel industry into what it is today. Corporate and incentive travel groups can be a profitable market. Searching out agencies that specialize in these types of markets could possibly add to your chances for building a rounded business.

Do your homework. Be creative when you are searching for income through a certain source. Don't you think corporate and incentive groups might like to cruise? Of course they do. When you do a ship inspection you will find group space dedicated to this kind of bookings.

Turn on your brainpower and those creative juices. Reach out and examine new brain waves, thoughts and ideas as you explore the world of today. We continue to call this thinking outside the box in any field. My travel career is still being built in much the same way – I continually explore new options, new opportunities. One of the key components to being successful in any career is to constantly be on watch for what is going on in the industry, keep the education process alive and situate yourself so you are moving in the same direction.

Since we are exploring the travel and cruise field here, always continue to ask yourself questions like "Who do I know in the travel/tour business? What are my connections in the scenic areas of the country/world? What experience do I already have that might lead me toward a new path or direction? What kinds of travel experience did I receive as a child, going through college or with past jobs? What talents do I have that might lead to a specialty product in the travel field? What can I do with my technical mind? How would that benefit me?"

AAA COLORADO

When AAA Colorado invited the trained Ports of Call professionals to join their group travel efforts, once again cruising came back on my radar screen. Again my thoughts went to "*What can I **give** that will give back in return?*" I volunteered to work in the Denver AAA office and worked creatively with others when working on projects.

When assigned a job, I worked closely with staff to duplicate information for the members. While attending AAA functions for the community, I became familiar with representatives from cruise lines and learned more about their companies.

My personal love of cruising must have been evident as I was chosen as a Cruise Host for several of the distinguished AAA CO President's Cruises. Slowly but surely my love of the industry turned into creation of a desired position. <u>L</u>ove <u>U</u>ntil <u>C</u>reation <u>K</u>nocks... L-U-C-K.

Both Steve Saey, Past President of AAA CO and Tony DeNovellis, current President of AAA CO, have expressed appreciation for the way in which having a professional Cruise Host aboard when entertaining groups enabled them to spend more time with clients in a relaxed atmosphere.

Joyce Saey and Judy DeNovellis, wives of those presidents, have also expressed positive opinions about their experiences cruising as "First Lady." They, too, were able to see how a more relaxed atmosphere for the leaders, without the anxiety of having to take care of all the details, was more conducive to spending time as it should be spent – with the clients.

Even though working as a Cruise Host on the President's Cruise was an annual event, other cruises and land tours kept me busy while I continued to be open to new opportunities.

AAA NORTHERN CALIFORNIA

An interview with Lynn Bowe of AAA CA, San Francisco, paved the way to an exciting Tahiti Cruise in 2003, the first of many cruises with the Northern California agency. My work with the local AAA had paid off.

One particular day sticks in my mind when Sandra Barnes in the AAA CO office called. Though I don't remember the exact words she used, the thought was clear: How soon can you pack for a cruise to Tahiti on the Tahitian Princess? My immediate reply was, "Give me fifteen minutes to pack and I'll be ready!" I must say I felt like a Princess myself – being on a Princess "Love Boat" as one of the Cruise Hosts. My L-U-C-K was paying off.

Incentive, as well as Customer Appreciation Cruises rank high in the AAA market, and various cruises required more than one Cruise Host. Some fond memories come to mind with over 300 guests and three Cruise Hosts arranging gifts in one small cabin. Needless to say there were a few giggles going on while trying to work around each other and keep track of who got what! The group communion brought flashbacks from the old Ports of Call days as my Cruise Host duties expanded.

CRUISE LINES/ITINERARIES/MOVING ON

In Chapter 6 you will learn about the International Tour Management Institute which afforded me opportunities to work for other Tour Operators, and I interspersed other cruises in and amongst the AAA assignments. The Delta Queen Steamboat Company had a huge presence in the group travel market, and I traveled with groups on all their Mississippi River itineraries from Minneapolis to New Orleans – as well as almost all their other river tributaries such as the Cumberland and Ohio. Once I was even stranded when the Ohio River rose to the point the boat could not go either direction. That turned out to be quite a vacation for those onboard.

Interestingly enough, these riverboat experiences paved the way for the upcoming and very popular European riverboat market of today. When first asked to host a group on Viking River Cruises from Budapest to Nuremberg with a coach continuing on to Prague, it brought back old times – much "older" history than the various stops in the United States for sure.

Cruises for numerous Tour Operators were on various cruise lines such as Crystal, Holland America Line, Royal, American Hawaii,

Pearl, Epirotiki, Princess, Celebrity, Royal Caribbean, and Norwegian to name a few.

Itineraries included both coasts of Mexico including Cancun/Cozumel; from Manzanillo to Cabo as well as the Mexican Riviera several times; East Coast U.S. and Canada twice; Bermuda twice; all areas of the Caribbean numerous times; Scandinavia combined with Russia, England and Germany; numerous trips through the Panama Canal; China; and Greece – as well as several cruise and land tours in Alaska including the Inside Passage. Combined with the Antarctica and Tahiti mentioned earlier, cruising replaced the "just" as I gained more experience on land and sea.

EXERCISES

1. Has education or additional training in your field sparked an interest you might like to pursue?
2. Does a particular passion continue to creep into your thought process as you explore employment options or work in your present environment?
3. Have you considered meditating repeatedly about a certain passion or skill you would like to pursue? If not, try going to a quiet space and sit with various ideas awhile. The process can be quite an eye opener.
4. Would you like to pursue Cruise Hosting as a career?

CHAPTER 6

CASE STUDY #1 – ITMI

While working for Ports of Call 'in the good old days,' the idea that perhaps some additional training in the travel field kept plaguing me until I found some answers. The following is an introduction to ITMI – my lifeline to the work I continue to love.

Terri, our youngest daughter, was living in San Francisco in 1993, so I stayed with her and took the intensive, two-week training class including field training that ITMI offered at the time.

Brooke Shannon paved the way for training in the Cruise Host field and taught a short class from her book entitled "Cruise Hosting." Her inspiring experience and love of the industry made me know I was in the right place at the right time. We also share the Shannon name.

As someone who has seen much of the industry, I share the following case study as an interesting example of what happens when two individuals with passion and a sincere desire to help others set out to reinvent an industry they love. Their hard work and determination, coupled with constantly keeping an eye on the industry itself, helped build a successful business.

And their ingenuity all relates to travel. Why did this particular business example impact my career so much? First read about them, then you can learn more of my secrets.

INTERNATIONAL TOUR MANAGEMENT INSTITUTE, INC. (ITMI)

Ted Bravos and William Newton, PhD, are known as pioneers of Tour Director/Cruise Host training in the tour and travel industry in the United States.

As each worked with individual styles for several Tour Operators, they soon found a common interest in their determined effort to have tour directing become known as a respected profession, much the same as professional guides are viewed abroad.

In 1976 Ted and Bill founded the International Tour Management Institute, Inc., in San Francisco, California. Bill's dry wit and sense of humor was complimented by Ted's charm and 'straight man' approach. Their years of experience and personal stories shared with students reduced the anxiety of intense training in the classroom and made learning fun.

Building on the respect they had for each other, they also built respect in the industry and ITMI soon became known for their quality Tour Director/Cruise Host graduates.

ITMI TODAY

Though Bill passed away in 2002, Ted and his dedicated staff continue to hold a number of ITMI training classes. Two-thirds of the training is in a classroom environment while the other one-third is hands-on training onboard a motor coach where participants get microphone experience. In 2010 most classes were held in San Francisco while an alternate location was Los Angeles, CA, at various times of the year.

Additionally ITMI hosts an annual symposium in a different geographical location every year. At the symposium Tour Operators and Tour Directors come together with a common purpose – interviewing and hiring. It is also a venue for continuing education and exchange of ideas as well as business and social networking. This event is a one-of-a-kind exposure for travel professionals.

Before and after each Symposium participants are offered complimentary pre- and post-sightseeing tours of the area while exchanging information with other Tour Director/Cruise Hosts and Tour Operators.

ITMI also offers educational field trips in other parts of the country at various times of the year. Even with the busy and time-consuming planning/teaching concepts described above, Ted Bravos still manages to travel as a Tour Director. In short, he continues on the path that drives his passion.

TRAINING TRAVEL PROFESSIONALS

Why were Ted and Bill so adamant about training professional Tour Directors and Guides? They loved to travel and teach others what they had learned themselves. Professionalism is key.

They both observed and studied the travel world, and they agreed that their students would be trained to represent the industry in the same passionate way in which they themselves performed.

Tour Operators are accustomed to hiring from a bank of ITMI graduates. Why? Because they know they can depend on the graduate being well trained and ready to go out in the field at any given notice.

When a Tour Operator hosts a busy season (like Fall foliage, for example) where unusually high volumes of people are traveling to the same locations and problems occur frequently, they need to know their Tour Directors are (1) well trained and (2) capable of handling unforeseen challenges.

AMBASSADORS OF PEACE

International travel is commonplace and a huge market in the Tour Directing/Cruise Host world. Early on the founders of ITMI recognized that travel abroad represents who most of us are: peace-abiding citizens. They felt, and still feel it necessary, for participants in ITMI classes to understand why his/her role as an 'Ambassador of Peace' plays an important part of life's journeys in today's tourism world. Sitting in ITMI class, I was surprised – they were using my term, too!

We need to remember our role as it relates to peace and goodwill as we reach out to touch others while representing our country and our values. Not only does ITMI teach how to deal with unruly clients who cause problems while on tour in their own country, but they also teach how to deal with groups traveling abroad. Graduates leave training with a firm understanding they are representing a universal concept, that of being an 'Ambassador of Peace' both at home and abroad.

Ironically enough, I found another niche that thinks like I do. As stated earlier, I had already *crowned myself* with the same title. In 1993, I found another home in the cruise/travel world as I embraced their teaching. It fit me as I confirmed once again: I'm in the right place at the right time.

Did ITMI come to me? No, I had to seek it out. I had to react to that kick start of uncertainty in the beginning, that fear of venturing into the unknown, step out of my boundaries and be convinced the ITMI training would rock my world. Not only did ITMI rock my world then, but it also continues to do so today.

ITMI'S ROLE IN MY LIFE

Remember that pivotal phone call that led me to years of Cruise Hosting for the AAA located in Northern California? I was offered that first Tahiti Cruise in part because of an interview I had where? – at an ITMI Symposium! When Lynn Bowe started a search for a Cruise Host for that particular cruise, not only did my resume come up on top of her interview folder from an ITMI Symposium, but the connection was also made through my local office in Colorado. Yes, some secrets of my success are in part documented through those ITMI channels.

And what about today? This year, ironically enough, I'm somehow experiencing yet another interesting "peace" tap on the shoulder from the latest ITMI Symposium held in January in Atlanta, GA. One of the keynote speakers, Sandy Dhuyvetter, Executive Producer of TravelTalkMEDIA in San Francisco, CA, is heavily involved in the role tourism plays in contributing to a more peaceful world. As she spoke about the subject matter this year, do you think I once again connected with the hat I wear as an 'Ambassador of Peace?' Absolutely!

Every year I attend Symposium, something sparks my creative mind that assures me I am in the right place at the right time. It's about that *inner* feeling of peace that comes when you feel as though you are part of a greater cause. In fact I always go home thinking: so THAT is the reason I was supposed to attend Symposium this year.

ITMI has been instrumental in my life because I am convinced I am, indeed, on the road to my highest good – on the road to what I was placed on this earth to do. Is there any better place I would rather be? I don't think so.

FEAR IN CHANGE

Even with my microphone experience on the airplanes, and my role as Tour Director/Cruise Host with POC, I still felt my knees shaking when I got up to present in front of my ITMI class during training. I'm sure you can relate to times when your knees felt a bit wobbly, too, especially when a peer group sits in the audience. Sometimes it happens when we least expect it.

Years later, with a lot more experience under my belt, I can now share some secrets about addressing fears that affect us at various times. I do have more ideas as we continue on our adventure. Shall we think about fear in the next part? I think it's a good idea.

EXERCISES

1. Have you considered outside occupation-associated training? If so, what has held you back in pursuing such training?
2. Can you think of some training that you feel might rock your world?
3. One of the biggest fears humans experience is that of speaking in front of an audience. Would ITMI help that?
4. As you begin to identify your own fears, are you afraid to face them?
5. Do you feel you are on the road to your highest good?

PART III

FEAR OF CAREER CHANGE

CHAPTER 1

ADDRESSING FEARS

～

Isn't it amazing how a four-letter word like **fear** can play such a huge role in a human being's life? Webster's definition of fear is *'alarm and agitation caused by expectation or realization of danger.'*

It is often said we fear failure and we fear success. That statement is certainly true as it relates to career change. It's the unknown that can keep our mind centered on shifting sand rather than solid ground. Change is always difficult in a questioning world of unknown and lack of familiarity.

What happens **if?** What happens **when?** What happens **where? How** will I cope? **What** will I do? **Who** will it affect? I've come to realize **facing the fear** is the biggest challenge in life as the waves of uncertainty unfold.

CHAPTER 2

SECRETS CONCERNING CAREER CHANGE

Career paths are an interesting phenomenon. I experienced at least one significant career alteration in my teens, 20's, 30's, 40's, 50's and now 60's. Perhaps my winding detours may give food for thought as you contemplate your own career path. The following is a short synopsis:

- Teens – Got married after 1 year of college and worked to put husband through veterinary school.
- 20's – Had 2 daughters. Three family moves. Worked at home while husband earned advanced degree.
- 30's – Two more family moves. Earned a business degree from University of Northern Colorado. Lost my Dad. Significant career changes for husband. Worked with husband in starting a new consulting business.
- 40's –Started working for Ports of Call Travel Club. Became a mother-in-law.
- 50's – Executive Producer of a CD entitled "Peace" after my first inspirational trip to the Holy Land. (More on that in Part V.) Another son-in-law; Mom failing; marriage flailing. Became a grandmother.
- 60's – Lost my Mom. Divorced after 41 years of marriage. Two more moves. Became an author.

Change is hard. Period. Career change is monumental.

Though some physical moves may cause a period of unsettledness, it's the mental moves that sometimes cause us the most anxiety. In both the physical and mental aspects of relocation or trying something entirely new, I've found the lack of familiarity seems to rock the boat. To reinforce my sense of security in the most anxious of times, I found it helpful to make a list of my qualifications.

To my pleasurable surprise I discovered strengths, talents and abilities that I hadn't made time to nurture when I transitioned from what I felt was "just a housewife and mother" to long-term career:

Nurse
Caretaker
Counselor
Administrator
Accountant
Promoter
Sales Person
College Graduate
Daughter
Best Friend
Community Service Volunteer
Spiritual Guide
PTA Supporter
Meal Planner, Shopper, Baker
Tennis Coach
Healer
Listener
Writer
Balloon Blower Upper (I threw that in for kicks.)
Confidante
CEO, Chief Executive Officer
CFO, Chief Financial Officer
Shepherd
Motivational Speaker
Organizer
Guide
Problem Solver

Gate Keeper
Disciplinarian
Entertainer
Event Planner
Personal Shopper
Photographer
Electrician
Plumber
Policewoman
Security Officer
Secretary
Taxi Driver
Gardener
Fearless Leader
Julie on Love Boat

Julie on Love Boat? Okay, so I had never actually **been** Julie on Love Boat – except in my mind. But I did always want to **be** Julie since the first day I met her on that old black and white Hallicrafter television in the farmhouse where we lived. That was my vision.

Now think about yours.

Ultimately it is a lot more palatable to envision yourself as Robert Kiyosaki – who is an expert on building wealth – than it is to think of yourself living under a bridge. That is exactly why I envisioned myself as Julie on Love Boat rather than imagining myself in a homeless shelter. Julie fit my personality.

Have you ever heard of a dream board? If not, perhaps it's time you tried one. It's pretty simple. Just start with a cheap corkboard where you post pictures of what you see in your future. Dream it. Speak it. Write it. Then live it. What you put out just might come back. Julie was always part of my dream, and my dream came true through my philosophy of L-U-C-K.

Sitting and listing all of the various jobs and responsibilities I had experienced in my life so far granted me what I needed, a sense of confidence in the process of career change. Positive reinforcement never hurt anyone.

Writing somehow gave me insight. Self-help books gave me a sense of moving forward while I searched for each new "me" that emerged. Dream boards kept my dreams alive and encouraged me to contemplate what was out there somewhere waiting.

Those types of exercises helped me as I continued to chart unknown waters throughout my life. Revisiting my long forgotten attributes helped me as I continued along life's journey while meeting every new crisis and every new career challenge.

Dream board! Dream board! Dream board! Who or what is a Julie for you?

EXERCISES

1. What qualifications can you list?
2. How does each give you a sense of encouragement?
3. What's on your dream board?

CHAPTER 3

F-E-A-R

Career change can be frightening or it can be considered adventurous and exciting. So many of the things we do in life center around attitude. But when major changes occur, sometimes the attitude takes second place to simply trying to reason what would be best for our future. Then that familiar word called fear pops up.

Let's focus for a moment on the timeframes listed for my changes. Fulfilling my role as supporting partner and mother led me through our early years together. The pressures of deciding what to do next was basically on the breadwinner's shoulders, however the uncertainty associated with family moves and changes fell on the partnership of marriage.

Change in family structure, family moves and growing daughters led me to the intense desire for higher education. I began to feel that gnawing discomfort within, leading me back to school for a college degree. That decision led to uncertainty and heightened fear. Was it fear of failure or fear of success? It was probably a bit of both.

Having had one year of college classes before marriage, I soon learned going back to a study regime as an adult with home responsibilities was a whole new ballgame. Women are known for multitasking, and the term took on a whole new meaning for me.

At this time of uncertainty obtaining a diploma was completely filled with fear, heightened anxiety and trepidation. I remember sobbing over a "D" grade while thinking I would never graduate. To an A/B student of what seemed like light years earlier, the embarrassment of a "D" was worse than the actual event. What we expect of ourselves can be monumental and I learned a hard lesson. In short: what will be will be.

Sometimes lowering expectations is okay. Here I was, a grown woman who could handle anything at home but not at all certain about a grade that really didn't matter in the grand scheme of things anyway. I did finally graduate.

When the girls were both settled into their own college careers, then came my exposure to travel that was another big adjustment on the home front. As I had always been 'chief cook and bottle washer,' significant changes necessarily took place as it related to household duties.

I even allowed the fear of my becoming irrelevant to the household structure cause me stress. Anticipation of an outcome (if we allow it) can cause unnecessary discomfort.

Later, when I suddenly found myself producing a CD brought about by a life-changing travel experience in the '90's, again frightening change resulted from all angles. I took on full responsibility of the necessary interactions with a new world of unknown such as attorneys, copyrights and the foreign world of music. In that process I again faced the fear of failure and fear of success.

Obviously the most impactful of the life-changing events occurred later, when I experienced a major year of shipwreck. Many of you will relate when I say I lost my anchor when my Mom passed away at 94 years of age. Mom was my absolute role model of positive reinforcement. My parents had experienced great heartache in their lives. Buddy, the brother I never knew, died in my mother's arms of whooping cough at two years of age, before penicillin was invented. Years later two of their three healthy daughters were positively diagnosed with polio in 1946 before the Salk vaccine was invented.

I ran the highest fever but miraculously did not paralyze. Through it all Mom's mantra consistently remained the same: *'God never gives you more than you can handle.'*

DIVORCE AFTER AGE 60

Also in 2003 I lost my marriage (my longest career, which encompassed 41 years) and my best friend since age 13. The void was overwhelming and my identity was lost somewhere in the stormy seas of nothingness.

At the time I couldn't voice what plagued my character the most. Both the feeling of abandonment and grief were ever present then — and continue with me today, though time continues to heal. No matter what in life, time marches on. Whether one experiences loss through death or divorce of a loved one, the grieving process is significant — at least it was for me.

Some said it took courage to walk away from the marriage, but I disagree with that theory. My walk was one of survival. My health was deteriorating as panic attacks entered the picture and I felt lost at sea. During eight years of intense counseling (we used three different counselors during that period to try and bring understanding to various issues of disagreement), one might consider the visual of living in a cocoon. Each counselor brought to the table various professional insights as more and more light of understanding brought about the cracking open of the cocoon.

Once those cracks of understanding became wider and wider, more and more light is shed and things are brought out into the open. Once so much light is shed on the subject, it is impossible to stuff oneself back into the darkness of a previous way of life and seal the cracks. But the thought of new butterfly wings (so to speak) gave me a sense of hope. Meanwhile, however, I lost my role in life and felt like a failure but couldn't explain why. I was filled with fear and certainly mixed emotions about the outcome.

The relationship had been experiencing mechanical difficulties for several years and in the end I felt as though I had to get out and frantically row the lifeboat to survive or go down with the ship. As I said, I chose survival. Driving to the mountains, where we owned a townhome property used for rental, I welcomed a sense of security that at least was not totally foreign to me. As the townhome was not rented at the time, it became my place of solitude and comfort — my "home away from home."

I spent hours trying to digest why a sense of inner peace had escaped me, while continuing to travel and write in search of the same. As I watched the snow fly I was grateful for this time of rebirth and meditation where I spent almost a year before filing.

Not only was the commitment factor a huge issue for me but also the words of a familiar country song continued to play in my mind: *Stand By Your Man*. I hate the word divorce, always have and always will. For about thirteen years after the term divorce was initially used in our household, together we thought we could hold it together. But it didn't work for me. I couldn't go back into that cocoon.

In the grieving process I learned that grief breeds fear. I had never made decisions alone. My parents were there until my marriage at age eighteen, and after that there was always a two-party decision-making process in place. The hardest part was walking away with the gripping fear of realization overwhelmingly constant. How would I ever make it on my own?

Every decision I made was monumental, but every step I took gave me a stronger will to make it alone. The good thing about faith is one is never truly alone, however, and my faith stood by me with resounding force. Once again I had to face my fears head on as I examined my past, explored my present and tried hard to envision a future on my own.

Yet Mom's words of security continually sounded in my ear: *'God never gives you more than you can handle.'* Every time I heard those words, I felt my parents' love and knew I would survive. The question was how to deal with it.

EXERCISES

1. What significant changes in your life have brought about fear?
2. What positive resource(s) do you use to combat fear?
3. Can you relate to the cocoon? How?

CHAPTER 4

REPLACING F-E-A-R WITH L-O-V-E

I found while rowing frantically in the tumultuous waves of despair and grief, my bright-colored orange life vest of searching and understanding kept me afloat. It felt as though I was in a brick chimney filled with water. My life vest kept my head out as I searched the heavens above for answers while treading water below as fast as I could to stay afloat.

It was all rather surreal as I plodded through life in a sort of daze. I answered with certainty "Yes" when various persons, including our daughter Terri, asked if I believed I had made the right decision in leaving the marriage. I was in fact sure of my answer yet still struggled with explanation and understanding in my mind and heart.

One day, three years after divorce and struggling with a mindset I couldn't seem to move on, I once again sought counseling – having two, two-hour sessions in one week. This barely known counselor literally put all the pieces of the puzzle together for me. She took away the chains of bondage that held me captive and I felt immediate relief and release.

Ironically enough, after those two intense counseling sessions, I paused on a Friday to watch a rerun of an Oprah show where the wife of a 9/11 victim was on the stage with her daughter. Her daughter sat beside her saying almost word-for-word the same things our oldest daughter Traci had said to me while sitting on my couch just a short time before. At the end of the show, what I took from it was: the best way I can honor our marriage of 41 years is to be present in our children's and grandchildren's lives now and embrace a new way of life. My earthly "dam" broke, and I collapsed in a flood of tears at the same time the woman on t.v. did the same.

Miraculously the brick chimney fell away, the water rushed out and I was able to walk again on solid ground. I have never been hypnotized but have seen the process on stage when a snap of the fingers brought someone back to reality. That's the best way I could describe my experience.

She explained to me I had been living in a traumatic state for some time. Her explanation was that sometimes we build an invisible shield around ourselves for protection from the emotional world when we live in a state of trauma. It's like a protection from any more arrows that can shoot to harm you. Instead of an invisible shield as she described, mine was a chimney built by both trauma and fear. Now isn't that a fine pair?

When the bricks fell away and I took off my life vest, an instantaneous revelation and transformation took place. Traci, having voiced concern for my well-being only weeks before, was around me only a few moments later on when she exclaimed "Mom! You're back! You're back! I don't know what's happened but you are back!" It was that evident.

From that day forward I began to feel empowered by the experience. From that day forward I began to realize the possibilities for creating abundance are limitless. It felt as though my abundance was running over and I wanted to share it with everyone with whom I came in contact.

GRACE, COURAGE AND TIME

Looking back, I believe what I was taught is immeasurable grace. Because I worked hard at the diagnostic part, forgiveness came without question. Peace came within. An assurance that everything is working as it should for me and those I love profoundly came into my heart and soul. Acceptance and a sense of abundance through love followed.

I can attest to the fact that facing your fears along with identifying your passion brings courage into the next phase of your journey. Learning from the fear process is invaluable. As courage takes over, fear subsides. Immobilization turns into positive energy and you are on your way to success.

Another grand healer is time itself. At any age we can know one thing for certain. The more time we spend with any given situation the easier it becomes. Continuing to grow in knowledge and understanding about that same given situation is paramount. The key is to be objective about the circumstances.

Capitalize the word **Courage** while you look toward a horizon that holds a secure future if you believe in yourself. If you're a quitter, you'll never be a winner. Hold onto a belief you ARE a winner and you will BE one!

EXERCISES

1. How has courage helped you in life-changing events?
2. Do you believe freedom can come from experiencing fear? How?
3. Has time helped you heal from a devastating circumstance in your life? Have you moved on?

CHAPTER 5

A FORMULA FOR FEAR

༄

Fear can be immobilizing. It can stop you dead in your tracks and sit you on a porch swing when you have been traveling all over the world at the speed of sound.

Fear can convince you that you cannot walk through an airport because the buzz in your head is louder than the buzz of excitement in the air. I know and understand just how devastating and suffocating fear can be, until you learn how to deal with it.

You could call it transformation or reformation of thought. A formula that has worked for me since the day the bricks fell away and I felt free is:

> **F – Face it.**
> **E – Embrace it.**
> **A – Analyze it.**
> **R – Replace it with love.**

Nothing replaces medical assistance if you need it, but any and all mental reinforcements can help. Whoever discovered journaling and counseling hit a home run as far as I'm concerned. They both allow you to examine your deepest feelings and validate your actions and reactions. Those two things, coupled with the faith Mom instilled in us, helped keep me centered – along with encouragement and help from my family physician, other family members and friends.

Through the darkest grieving of those difficult times, I used writing and prayer as comfort food. I even slept with a Bible I carried to the Holy Land in 1996 when bombs went off and shook the hotel windows where our tour group stayed. Yet I still experienced a triumphant sense of peace while traveling there so I held that within reach.

REPLACING FEAR WITH LOVE

Today I realize how much the **F-E-A-R** formula means to me because I've successfully learned how to replace fear with love in many circumstances. I tell myself constantly there is not room for both. It's as simple as that.

When the over-powering feeling of **fear** suddenly starts to run through my brain, I take a deep breath and consciously replace it with **love.** It even goes back to the L-U-C-K we talked about before. I hold onto the LOVE Until Creation Knocks. The creative process of healing, when wrapped in love, can be immeasurable.

It's the same principle whereby we replace fear. Try it. Think of some circumstance that fills you with fear. You start to feel your body tense and your anxiety level raise. The fear of the fear can be immobilizing.

Now concentrate as you change the word fear to love. Mentally grab your security blanket, whatever that looks or feels like to you personally. Yours may be a tattered and worn blanket or stuffed toy you had as a child. Visually feel it in your hands. Love it.

My mind goes to that Bible I mentioned. It's covered in blue denim with a heart cross-stitched on the front. I feel the fabric and run my fingers over the shape of the heart. Just as the visualization of strength comes from the feel of the course denim fabric, I feel the fabric of my life being strengthened as well. I trace the heart, lovingly cross-stitched in the center on the front of the Bible and feel the love that gift represents. Both inside and out, that small yet magnanimous gift represents the word love itself. It is no secret the Bible teaches us about fear as stated in 1 John 4:18: Perfect love casts out fear.

Rather than an object, perhaps a person who gave you strength may pop into your mind. Feel that person's face and features as stepping out of your comfort zone became reality. There may be multiple persons who fill that vision. Whatever held you to the familiar can indeed create a healthy base for building a strong future as you take that first step toward freedom. Hold onto the positive as you eliminate the negative.

As you held and perhaps still hold tight to an unknown future as we all do at times, feel the security and love of that special someone or multiple someone(s) who represent a sense of confidence, a sense of wholeness and happiness, a sense of security in unfamiliar circumstances. Hold onto the love as you release the fear, letting it go as you feel the warmth of a puffy down-filled jacket on a cold and windy day.

Feel the anxiety wane as you begin to relax by holding on to that security blanket, that feeling of encouragement. After a more relaxed feeling, keep filling the space with more and more **love.** Are you squeezing out the word fear as you replace it with love? Is there room for both fear and love to occupy your brain at the same time? Believe it can work for you as you practice the exercise. It costs nothing to try it.

If you put fear into the universe, what do you get back? Fear. If you put love into the universe, you inevitably will get back love I promise you.

An example I can think of is the story of a woman being held at gunpoint by a robber. To overcome her own fear, she calmly started talking to the man about his grandmother in a kind and loving way.

As she continued to talk of ways in which her own grandmother had shown love, the robber began to back off his intensity. With the powerful interaction of the minds, he eventually gave himself up and thanked her for saving his life because she kept him from doing something he would always regret. Love is powerful.

Love, Love, Love until it fills every cell of the body, every pore of the skin, every bone in the skeleton and every particle of the blood in you. LOVE until creation knocks on your door and tells you how to beat down the bad guys and revel in your accomplishment. It can work.

One thing here is very important. **Love yourself.**

We all make mistakes and we all have opportunities to beat ourselves up. But if we dwell on the negative, the results can be disastrous. If we choose a higher road of forgiveness, love never fails.

Feeling the unfamiliar is not a bad thing. Note I did not say it is comfortable; I said the end result *can* be good. Working through the pain is part of the process of healing. Understanding the joy of truth is freedom in the making.

Every day we have a chance to grow from the tiny baby steps of uncertainty to the long strides of confidence. As a friend once said, "If you're going to win the race, you've got to take that first step toward the finish line." I found you've got to get into the lifeboat if you choose survival. And in the words of Mother Teresa, "Peace begins with a smile."

EXERCISES

1. What or who represents a sense of security to you?
2. Can you work at replacing fear with love?
3. Are you willing to try?
4. Can you replace the negative parts of your past with positive goals for your future?

CHAPTER 6

WHAT IS THE SECRET IN FACING FEAR?

Some secrets necessarily remain forever in the boundaries of a trust shared with another human being, while other secrets can be revealed when excitement abounds in the telling.

What is the secret of stepping out of your comfort zone, trying something new and wrapping your arms around a whole different future than you ever imagined? More of my secrets will be revealed in Part V, but for the moment let's look at some other personal stories that have led to success.

When I first heard the story of a woman named Juliet St. John, I was amazed. She gave up everything and lived in her car – to provide special education and training for her children. I cannot imagine how much fear accompanied her on that journey. Was it worth it, giving it all away to embrace an unknown future?

I personally watched this same woman walk across a stage in St. Louis, MO and accept a check for $1,000,000 – only a few years after the car experience. Anything is possible, no matter the age or stage in life, in our free country. If one is willing to work *at* success, it is possible to be a success. Juliet has an eighth grade education.

It's not about the money – Juliet doesn't need more millions. It's about the millionaire giving from her heart – giving 100+ percent of her time and energy to insure others' success. She's always searching for just five or six more hours in each day to encourage others to change lives through YTB/ZamZuu, the company that gave her a chance – a chance to pay for her son's education, provide for her daughter and her mother, and travel the world.

The monetary rewards are great and provide for various luxuries, but Juliet will tell you today her greatest reward is seeing her children thrive. She was one proud mother as she recently sat and watched her son walk across his own stage to receive a Master's Degree with honors. According to Juliet, her pride rests in what HE accomplished and what her daughter has accomplished.

As I said before, my first amazement was in hearing her story about living in the car – but the amazement part doesn't stop there. I recently received an e-mail from Juliet about her personal fears – one of which was the terrifying notion she would jump off the largest Bungy jump in New Zealand, in part because her son Max encouraged her to do so. She shared she is both claustrophobic and scared of heights, and the toughest part was making the decision to try the terrifying feat (while experiencing vertigo I might add).

Photographs accompanied the extreme venture as she proved both to her son and to HERSELF she could overcome the fear and do it! Wrapping up the scenario in her words: the feeling of freedom and sense of accomplishment is the best thing in the world. She now uses that experience to help others overcome their fears – yes, she is one amazing woman indeed.

Whatever fear accompanied Juliet while living in that car was totally replaced by the L-O-V-E she continues to show for her own family, as well as her YTB/ZamZuu family. Read about the company that gave her that chance in Case Study #2.

CASE STUDY #2, YTB/ZAMZUU

When Lloyd Tomer was sixteen years old, his mother called her four children into the bedroom where she lay contemplating the immediacy of her death. She pointed to each of the brothers and sisters of Lloyd and described what their life's journey would look like. Each of those job descriptions has indeed played out exactly as she predicted they would.

When she came to Lloyd, she told him God had something special in mind for him, a special purpose that would change the country and he would have to search for it. Since that day he kept that vision alive and started on his own journey of discovery.

In 2001 J. Lloyd Tomer, his son Scott Tomer, and a trusted insurance company associate J. Kim Sorensen founded YourTravelBiz.com. They based the company on the same honesty and integrity they had learned from A. L. Williams, the insurance company that brought Lloyd Tomer from a one-room shack to an income in the millions as he faced his reality and turned his life around.

Today YTB International, Inc. is a publicly traded company that has seen its ups and downs as "Coach" (as he is known today) continued to follow his "vision" created by his mother.

"Coach" Tomer's vision and the inception of YTB is poignantly presented in his book "The 4th Quarter." Published in 2009, Coach Tomer explains founding YourTravelBiz.com in 2001 along with his partners J. Kim Sorensen and his son Scott Tomer.

As stated on his book cover, Coach is "An ordinary man with an *Extraordinary Drive* to change the world. His motto: 'Quitters never win, and winners never quit.'" Isn't that the truth? That is another point I have tried to make throughout this book. Though the journey may be filled with uncertainty, winners never quit.

I use these three businessmen as an example because they never gave up in the face of adversity, just as Coach had experienced in that one-room shack. Determined to be winners, Coach's vision keeps them on track in the business world. I believe my mom's vision keeps me on track as well.

THE INTERNET WORLD

Using their experience in the world of insurance and seeing the travel industry turn toward the Internet, the three founders launched a word-of-mouth Internet-based travel and referral marketing company using the concept "people helping people." Together they invested millions of dollars to build a base on which to stand and on which to become recognized in the travel world.

Starting in 2001, YTB rode the dynamic wave of what's known as a market shift in the travel industry. As consumers became more and more comfortable with booking travel online, profits soared and YTB flourished. As I researched the company I learned Kim Sorensen was becoming known in the travel world by 2007, just six years after YTB was started. It appears the founders were making headway by becoming known in the industry —jumping out of the box and forging ahead in the fast-paced world of change caused by the Internet. And for the record, they were not always popular because of it.

Around 2007-2008 the idea of "baby boomer travel" and growth in E-Commerce became common subject matter as home-based businesses continued to grow in popularity, particularly in the travel agent community. Brick and mortar retail stores, along with struggling travel agencies found the new "click and mortar" way of doing business on the Internet a whole new world to understand and comprehend. Changes started taking place rapidly as Internet sales escalated.

Today over $80 million in travel commissions have been paid out to YTB home-based travel store owners. YTB has received awards from cruise lines such as Carnival, Princess and Holland America Line as well as from Tour Operators like Trafalgar, Funjet, Sandals, Globus Family of Brands and Apple Vacations.

Dr. Marc Mancini, a well-known and respected name in the travel industry, developed the YTB online training modules for travel agent training through a site owner's travel portal. One of the things YTB is best noted for is the extensive travel training available online. Awards such as those listed above demonstrate how site owners have taken advantage of various methods of learning. Travel sales continue to be on the upswing, even in today's economy.

I cite YTB as an example of what is happening in the Internet travel/cruise industry, because the company has weathered what seemed like insurmountable storms — while helping a significant number of people in need. Many success stories have surfaced through the company's success. There may be other internet-based travel companies out there, but I am yet to find another business of this type that has pulled through so many trials and come out a winner after only ten years in business.

ZAMZUU

As the economy plummeted, YTB's trials escalated. Several of the top income-producing directors left for other business pursuits, thinking the grass would be greener elsewhere. A huge lawsuit in California cost the company in dollars, but ironically enough paved the way for continued success. Coach's vision never wavered.

As they felt the pain of humans floundering in tough economic conditions, the founders searched for and hired key people. By strategizing a way to weather the storm, they knew they could help those in need. YTB became stronger – in part because of the dedicated directors who remained loyal and worked even harder.

In January, 2010 YTB founders Tomer, Sorensen and Tomer made a big announcement. With history on their side in analyzing trends in the marketplace, YTB International launched a total E-Commerce Center, where site owners could expand their travel businesses and catch the Internet shopping market shift on the way up.

ZamZuu was born as a result. When an individual becomes associated with ZamZuu, that person essentially has his/her own retail shopping mall and travel center. The ZamZuu site is given a name by the person who created the account. Retail stores pay commissions on purchases made through a ZamZuu store.

Retail stores quickly jumped onboard, including such familiar names as Macy's, Nordstroms, Best Buy, Old Navy, Sears, ToysRUs, BabiesRUs, Kohl's, Sports Authority, MacMall, Omaha Steaks, Sports Authority, iTunes, Walmart, Target, Sears and Sam's – to name a few of the hundreds of stores found on a ZamZuu website.

Some think recognized store names like Circuit City are no longer in business, when in actuality they have simply turned to the Internet for sales. It stands to reason we will see more and more stores head in the same direction as many popular stores now offer rewards for shopping through their Internet sites.

"Specialty Stores" also line up to join ranks with this Internet E-Commerce venture, as owners report increased sales from added exposure through ZamZuu site owners and their business associates. Once again it appears the 'people helping people' motto is getting used in multiple ways. It's like one big family.

ZAMZUU CONVENTION, AUGUST 2010

In preparation for their annual Convention, Lloyd Tomer once again called a meeting of the founders to brainstorm yet another visionary idea, "Instead of a franchise where we **charge** big bucks to join," Coach said, "why don't we **give stores away**? We need to continue to reach out to those in need."

At the 2010 Convention, the new business plan was introduced. Citing the example of AOL that gave hundreds of thousands of disks away to publicize the company, the founders established the term FREE AGENT and started giving away shopping mall/travel stores. It costs nothing to sign on and establish a shopping/travel store as a Free Agent – in return the agent receives 30% of the commission paid for purchases made in their online business.

If a person wants to participate in giving Free Agent sites away, he/she must purchase a BROKER license. Further if a person wants to build a networking business, there is no cost to become a REP who sells the license.

Then, Free Agents were given the opportunity to expand into the already established YTB Travel Network that has been the consistent moneymaker for YTB International, Inc. By taking "First Class Training," the Free Agent can potentially increase their income and become more knowledgeable in the travel industry.

By allowing Free Agents to make increased commissions paid on travel plus have more exposure to the travel income potential, the founders demonstrate the fact they intend to "keep on giving." Personally talking with various participants in this business world gave me confidence in the fact money can be made in the cruise industry through YTB/ZamZuu. Read on.

A PROFESSIONAL CRUISE HOST ROLE

"And just how does this affect me, looking at a possible career as a professional Cruise Host?" you ask. For the answer to that question, let me introduce you to a couple of women who represent YTB/ZamZuu.

Jeanie Sharpless ... Sometimes referred to as a "Travel Queen" Director with YTB, Jeanie Sharpless is a spirited example of how the company has changed her life. In her words, "I've never had more fun, helped more people or earned more income than I have with YTB/ZamZuu. I love to tell people 'I'm not in it – It's in ME. It is my mission to give the best 'gift' I can ever give by pointing people to this business because it truly keeps on giving."

I asked Jeanie a few questions that follow here.

CLM: "How did you get started with the company?"

"My husband Bill questioned me when I suggested joining a company where we could 'get paid to travel' while generating multiple streams of income and paying for three children in college at the same time. In fact when I suggested taking money from the budget to fly to St. Louis and meet the founders of YTB, Bill said something like 'Woman, are you out of your mind?!!" That's a direct quote!

"But thankfully he agreed to go as it was important to the both of us to make sure YTB was a company of individuals with integrity that would not tarnish our name in any way. When we met Coach we instantly felt a connection that demonstrated all we had hoped for and more. We have never looked back as we joined his team and his dream while establishing an even bigger 'family' of our own. Because of Coach, Scott and Kim's dedication, commitment and strength, our business is thriving today."

CLM: "I've talked to some people who have home-based businesses who mentioned having more freedom. What does the word 'freedom' mean to you in your business, Jeanie?"

"I never went to college and quite frankly never dreamed of getting paid for all the freedoms we enjoy…..Freedom of Time, Freedom of Financial Worry, Freedom to Vacation while indeed 'getting paid,' Freedom of knowing our children are taken care of through a Copyrighted Bill of Rights and inheritable business, and Freedom of included health and life insurance benefits. In six months we were making more than any 9 to 5 employer would ever pay me. YTB was and is a dream come true."

CLM: "What about training? Does the company offer training?"

"To keep our team plugged in, we constantly discuss the variety of training opportunities available through conference calls, trade shows, webcasts, news updates from our home office support about the travel industry and vendor webinars. Folks will only stay tuned in if they are plugged in, educated and motivated while seeing results."

CLM: "So Jeanie, the sparkle in your character jumps out when you speak about your work as it relates to travel in general. I'm wondering how cruising fits into the over-all picture for you and your team?"

"Building on cruises teaches the commission process and it teaches how to earn large sums of money quickly. Cruise training is actually what I concentrate on with a new business partner because it is a multitude of travel trainings wrapped into one. It teaches agents the importance of relationship marketing, networking and building retention. It teaches how to work all aspects of the travel business and how to work directly with vendors.

"Booking a few group cruises every year has the potential to pay better than what most people earn at a 9-to-5 job. There is no limit to the number of cruises I can book, and there is no limit to the amount of income I can earn for the work I do. And I don't have to 'clock in and clock out.'

"The neat part about cruising is I can cruise with my clients or book cruises FOR my clients. Either way it's a win/win deal. Plus it is 'word-of-mouth advertising' for my business. Who doesn't want to take a cruise? If you do a good job at 'Customer Service' the first person tells many more, and your business continues to grow."

CLM: "Jeanie, your infectious enthusiasm is evident. Here is one last question for you. Can anyone 'make a living' using YTB/ZamZuu as a source for cruising into their own future?"

"Absolutely anyone can make a good living at booking cruises. Cruises are the best travel bargain out there. More importantly we can make a difference in people's lives by putting together dream cruises and promoting them to anyone and everyone. It's not all about making money. This business pays us well to 'make dreams come true' and can make career income a reality. If you want to do it part-time or full-time, the choice is yours.

"As a travel professional, we learn quickly that group cruises offer the best income opportunity and therefore impact and benefit our business the most. I'm proud to say that cruising IS my business. I'd also like for you to talk with someone I call the 'Cruise Queen,' Mary Cofield. Mary is a great example of someone who took cruising to a whole new level through her teaching. She has taught several National Convention training sessions in St. Louis."

I was fascinated with all the information from my first interview, so immediately I called the telephone number Jeanie gave me. Here is what I learned: After working as an agent for the Internal Revenue Service for thirty years, Mary Cofield saw the obvious **tax** benefits of becoming a referring travel agent with YTB and having a home-based business after she retired. She had discovered the joy of travel while employed by the IRS and loved the diversity of people, climate, culture, geography and architecture that the United States offered.

Establishing her business with YTB, international travel lured her into the cruise market because of the ease of waking up in a new location with each port stop. She became hooked on cruising and the luxuries it affords while realizing a whole new income stream.

"Cruising is one of the best values during a rough economy," Mary says. "I quickly discovered that first-time cruisers and 3-day getaways were the best volume sales for my travel business at this point in the economy. My business didn't suffer because I adjusted my product to fit the times.

"Within my YTB Travel site, I also used any slow periods to increase my cruise knowledge by taking classes online and earning certification as an Accredited CLIA (Cruise Lines International Association) Cruise Counselor (ACC). This certification requires cabin sales, ship inspections and completion of product knowledge courses.

"I took my knowledge and then developed workshops and helped my other team members learn what I learned as a cruise coordinator. That's what I love about the YTB business model: it benefits me to show my team what I learn and enables me to help them grow, too.

"'People helping people' is what I like best about YTB as my host agency. The founders and staff encourage me and allow me to grow and help others grow with me. I love that! Now my team specializes in group cruises and earns money from group sales, in addition to working the marketing side of the business if they choose. There are no quotas and no inventory. Everyone can work the business as much or as little as they want, but my team has found so many advantages in cruising they keep it up. Cruising gets in your blood and it makes you money.

"I usually get repeat business at least three times from a group. It amazes me how a simple amenity such as a tote bag or bottle of wine means so much to the clients. They remember the extras. I usually join my cruise groups, especially the first-time cruisers, so I can plan onboard activities. Even though there are many activities onboard, they still like group events and outings planned as a group. That's the fun in it all.

"I have a motto for my team: 'Recruit and Cruise Your Way to Success.' Directorship in YTB/ZamZuu is my ultimate dream and anyone can join me in this quest. There are no limits for obtaining financial success with the company and with so many cruise ships sailing the oceans today, the market is wide open. It's all about setting a goal and making it happen.

"Retirement for me turned out to be much more rewarding than I ever thought possible. The fact I can help people makes it even better. I keep thinking this life is like being on a break *from* work when it is actually called work itself. It's a lifestyle people think is too good to be true – but sure enough it is true, as I am a living example. Now that my husband Roland is retired, we both work the travel profession as business partners. We have reverse roles; he is now the bookkeeper for the business and I'm the marketing specialist. No more tax work for me!"

It seems obvious that both Jeanie Sharpless and Mary Cofield have become accustomed to making their personal dreams come true. One question I failed to ask is if they watched Julie on Love Boat as I did growing up. I'll save that question for another time.

TAX CONSIDERATIONS

Tax considerations are always a focus when a new career possibility comes around –- another reason we often feel anxious in career change. After my interviews, I decided to go one step further and look into references on the subject matter – taxes.

What I found is a book entitled: "Home Business Tax Savings, Made Easy!" by Ronald R. Mueller, MBA, PhD. "It's How Much You Keep That Counts, Not How Much You Make" was the title of the first 4 editions of this same book, now in its 5th Edition. (The book and a lot of other free and lost-cost savings information are available at: www.HomeBusinessTaxSavings.com.) The knowledge I gained from this valuable resource surpasses anything I'd previously found on the subject of taxes. For starters, the above manuscript is the only plain-English guide to special home business tax deductions approved by Congress.

As training is also important in any field, I recently tuned into a conference call with Alan Horton, Denver-based Level I Director for YTB, who interviewed Author Ron Mueller. I had listened to him speak before, and once again found myself struggling to keep up with all the pertinent information given. Not trusting my skill at recording everything perfectly, I decided to call Dr. Mueller myself and confirm what he had said. After the follow-up call, Dr. Mueller sent me the following points by e-mail to be included here:

1. <u>**Taxes**</u> cost most Americans more than their housing, transportation, food and health care – **<u>COMBINED</u>**!

2. Home-Based business owners can qualify for more tax deductions than any other category of taxpayer, bar none.

3. Congress has approved dozens of tax deductions for the specific purpose of encouraging taxpayers to run home-based businesses because of the benefits to the American economy.

4. The two requirements to qualify are simply to work your business at least 3-4 hours a week, and to be *trying* to make a profit.

5. Just the SIX of those new deductions (the 6 with the biggest payoffs) can increase the tax REFUND of most taxpayers by $3,000 to $6,000 *or more*.

6. The additional refund can be collected throughout the year, at a rate of approximately $300-$500 per month — more than enough to cover the operating costs of most home-based businesses.

7. All six can be understood and put into use in about 4 hours.

Yes, I had heard correctly on all these seven points. The conference call was timely, as is the information shared. I knew Congress had made some changes regarding home-based business deductions, but confirming the information made it even more real. Like me, you may have to read the points several times for the information to completely sink in. Most of us simply take taxes for granted – not stopping to digest completely just how much we are affected in our daily lives – and/or in a weekly or monthly paycheck.

As pointed out in Dr. Mueller's information, it is evident I found yet another way to "get paid." We like getting paid, right?

FEAR OF CAREER CHANGE

I chose to join YTB after looking at various work possibilities where I could build residual income and provide something that is inheritable for our children and grandchildren as well. And of course I wanted to continue to cruise! That *inner* feeling – *the time has come to find additional ways to cruise rather than totally rely on outside sources* – started to dominate my thought processes. When "it" happened, I knew I could choose f-e-a-r in stepping outside my comfort zone again, or choose l-o-v-e in believing. The belief in myself solidified my decision and I chose the high road. It felt right.

Sitting in a class as part of 'YTB University,' I listened to a speaker who talked to a crowded classroom, filled with enthusiastic and questioning participants who were facing the fears of career change and recording information as fast as they could. It was an hour filled with anticipation and learning. It made me realize I could help hundreds of people by putting my experience down on paper. I needed to write a book – to share my years of Cruise Host and Tour Director knowledge. And so I set out to help as many people as I could. This book solidifies my efforts for over two years while continuing to build a business.

The business has grown as friends call, knowing I am now booking travel to places where I have been myself. Additionally YTB offered a guaranteed program of which I took advantage. I also took 1st Class Training plus Travel Agent Training to increase my percentages in commissions and am working on a CLIA (Cruise Line's International Association) certification. Cruises are the favorite part of my travel business and I continue to learn as I go.

Once again, getting paid comes in various ways. Always being available to my colleagues who need answers on different itineraries or cruise ships is a huge way to measure success. Writing a book is in itself an investment in the future. Have I received my check for $1,000,000 yet? Let's just say I'm working on it. The best is yet to come – *I know it inside!* After completion of the book, I'll soon be back to Mary Cofield's motto: Recruit and cruise your way to success.

Meanwhile on the YTB travel/cruise side of the business, getting paid is easy. Even though vendors have a full 90 days after a trip is complete to pay YTB, it's not uncommon to receive commission checks from YTB in about 3-4 weeks following a trip. At least, that has been my personal experience. The more travel you book, the greater the financial rewards. As in any business, it takes time and effort as you build.

The technical guide contained in Part I is available to all for training purposes. I'm excited to team up with cruise enthusiasts like Jeanie and Mary to do some training on the oceans of the world. Contact me at www.CarolLeeMiles.com/Training for more information. Perhaps we can all capitalize on both learning and getting paid at the same time. Did I mention I love my job? I meant to!

EXERCISES

1. Can you relate to living in a car or in a one-room shack?
2. What are your aspirations for "retirement"?
3. Have you thought about becoming a millionaire?
4. If so, how do you plan to go about it?
5. Have you set goals to achieve your next plateau, whatever that is?

CHAPTER 7

THE INTERNET AND PROFESSIONAL CRUISE HOSTS

∽

Opportunities for professional Cruise Hosts in today's market are out there. You have the opportunity to take your time and go search them out. If cruising is your passion, as mine is, you can find a way to make it happen.

Does it take work? You bet it does.

Can it become a full-time career? Yes, as pointed out by my interviews, there are ways to make that happen, too.

But don't stop there. Go out and find someone who can help you learn, someone who has climbed the ladder of success, and get an interview with that person yourself. Use that knowledge – and smile when you see a perfect score on your career change exam. Change your f-e-a-r to l-o-v-e and embrace a new way of thinking as you "go and grow."

How do you know they practice what they preach?

Here is a way to start. Attend regional meetings put on by the individuals involved, tour their offices and attend a company convention. Ask for financial records. If the company is publicly traded, these records are readily available. Continue to do your homework.

Additionally, it never hurts to talk with individuals who have been involved with a company for a number of years and ask them how they have been treated and what they think of the whole organization. Then make your own determination.

In other words, do your homework with an opportunistic yet objective approach. Do not always count on the opinions you read on the Internet. Remember that underlying motives can drive a person's purpose for slander. Be wary of unfounded statements that in reality hold no truth.

Look for the reputation and principals that feed your desire to be successful in your field. It may not be cruise hosting – but then again, perhaps it might be a good choice for you. Owning your own successful business at least gives you the freedom to make choices.

Nelson Mandela once said: "I learned that courage was not the absence of fear, but the triumph over it. The brave man is not he who does not feel afraid, but he who conquers that fear." (and I would add 'with love.')

EXERCISES

1. Can you replace FEAR with LOVE?
2. How would that benefit you in changing careers?
3. Are you living in an "out of money" world?
4. How can you correct that? Or make things better for you and your family?
5. Are you afraid of the Internet? Career change?
6. If so, how can you work on that?

PART IV

SECRETS OF CRUISE HOST PSYCHOLOGY

CHAPTER 1

SHARING STORIES

Psychology intrigues me. One of the most important secrets I have learned in the career of Cruise Hosting is that people in general want to share. They want to share their story. They want to sit with you and talk, feel your sincerity and walk away with the thought that someone cares.

No matter the age, no matter where they are in their life journey, they still want to share. This is especially true in the electronic world as we know it today.

When you consider how much time was spent in the "good old days" in communion with other human beings compared to today's world made up of cell phones, computers, commute time to and from work, texting, Facebook or Twitter, etc., you can understand the point I am making.

My family came together for square dancing, ice cream socials, children's performances at country schools, quilting bees, athletic events, helping with harvest or church potlucks. During or afterward it seems people had time for relaxed conversation and sharing.

I had never thought about that as compared to our lifestyle today until two guides from Guatemala asked me how in the world I could live in the U.S. with such intensity and anxiousness, always in a state of hurry and never a state of relaxation with time for family.

They had each worked for a time in the U.S. for the purpose of improving their English to become better tour guides. While living in California, they studied the culture and interacted in this society, one totally foreign to their own lifestyle. Each agreed it was like culture shock. They could not wait to get back to their home country.

I thought about that conversation as I began to try and educate myself in the world of psychology, studying people's actions and reactions. The guides were right about one thing. In one way or the other, clients are usually ready to leave the fast-paced anxiety that seems to plague almost every household these days, and welcome the relaxation of a cruise. Is it possible that cruising might fill a similar role to the gatherings I mentioned before? In the world of today group and family cruises continue to grow in number.

Cruise Hosts love the simple smiles and warm hearts in those folks that go about their days with no complaints and no problems, interacting at the parties, being spoiled with recognition and generally just hanging out. Those clients enjoy the atmosphere and basically do their own thing. They don't get upset when things aren't quite right; they roll with the punches and smile. We love those clients. They leave their worries behind and come along for their first cruise or their tenth or their hundredth. They seem to have that joy, joy, joy, joy down in their heart as the old song goes.

Over time I learned to listen more intently to stories. The Guatemala guide conversation enabled me to start looking deeper into the heart of an 89 year-old-man who can discuss living in horse and buggy days and share how his Jewish in-laws escaped a prison camp. It also led me to tune in more intently to the young adult who had already spent two years traveling India in search of his spirituality and next wants to ride a bicycle across the U.S.

Listen to their stories, even if some tend to repeat the same one over and over again. The psychology of listening and caring could easily be taught in any profession. Sincerity and understanding begins and ends with heartstrings of love.

EXERCISES

1. Are you a good listener?
2. Do you find listening too much of a bore in your fast-paced world?
3. What bores you about it? How could you become a good listener?
4. How has the Internet changed your every-day life?
5. Do you consider those changes positive or negative? Why?

CHAPTER 2

A TRUE FATHER AND SON STORY

☙

When one of my groups came together for a Pre-Cruise Party to Antarctica, a dad waited until other clients had left the room and asked me if I would be willing to share a confidence. He confided in me he had recently been diagnosed with a terminal disease, and he was keeping that information from his son who was to travel with him and share a cabin on the cruise.

Following the trip, his son was to accompany him on their one-hour drive back home, which is when he planned to tell him. My heart went out as this precious little man in his cute little French beret tam smiled at me as we embraced, with an understanding that would be shared on a 3-week journey to the Southern most area of the world. As he told his story, I tuned into his life.

The Antarctica journey could be described as surreal. Not only did it seem as foreign as "landing on the moon" but the surround sound of millions of penguins speaking at once seemed to bond our small group. Together we absorbed everything the fascinating guest lecturers had to say concerning the mostly ice-covered continent.

We slid down mountains of ice on a makeshift "sled," giggling like little school children out playing in the white wonderland, then interacted with Russians living there who wanted to share their vodka and sell us crafts.

I kept my antiquated camera busy taking snapshots of the group, but particularly concentrating on various poses of Dad as he contemplated his last days on this earth. I wondered what it must be like to be in that position and in many ways felt honored to share his *secret*.

There was a constant sense of peace surrounding Dad and me, each day sharing the warmth of quick hugs and knowing smiles. There was always that twinkle in his eye as we communicated without a word. The days continued in our own sense of oneness, rarely having a quiet moment alone for him to share his thoughts and feelings but when he did, I felt honored to listen.

In my mind I continued to praise the woman who lovingly sent the two "guys" off on their own journey to share their last time together even though she was giving up her own precious time. My thoughts encompassed yet another beautiful love story that had just been recorded in the annals of time.

I remember the flight home when I awoke in the night and walked to the back of the plane for some exercise. Dad reached out and grabbed my arm as I passed by his row. Not realizing anyone else was even awake at that hour, I stopped and was greeted with the same twinkle in his eye and smile on his face.

I wondered about his thoughts then of going home and literally how it must feel. We didn't have a chance to have a last conversation but he seemed to be in complete control when we arrived back in Denver at the terminal.

From the parking lot I watched as Dad and Son drove off together. Son was driving as Dad glanced back through the window and winked, smiling as his head bobbed in his French beret. The one-hour drive was to be filled with emotion and obviously I was, too. I could not contain the tears as I climbed into my car for my own drive home, realizing I might never see either of them again.

Son called me a few months later, sharing the news of his father's death and thanking me for the comfort and support his dad expressed he felt in a land so far away during that precious time of *secrets*. I told him a picture of him and his dad, perfectly placed in front of the cruise ship, was on its way.

The psychology of simply listening while actually filling the roll of a security blanket is not to be taken lightly. For this my payment has nothing to do with money, yet makes me feel incredibly wealthy all the same.

EXERCISES

1. Has the psychology of listening affected your life? How?
2. Are you good at keeping secrets? How would the father's secret have affected your trip?

CHAPTER 3

CHALLENGING CLIENTS

∽

Interactive relationships within the psychological boundaries of a traveling group can be challenging. But they can hold a sense of adventure, too, trying to analyze how things might turn out.

You'd think clients excited about a cruise itinerary and looking for a nice vacation or incentive trip would be content and happy for a week or more of fun in the sun or exploration to various parts of the world. But sometimes in what seems the best of circumstances, challenges still find a way to appear at the most unexpected moments.

Just as things are never perfect at home, the same is true when traveling. Perhaps the ship is having an issue with mechanical problems or an unexpected flight schedule change causes some anxiety for the trip home. The Cruise Host is ultimately the one who ends up dodging the bullets when the guns go off.

It took me years to learn it is not **personal** when the person who becomes angered places blame on me for whatever circumstance he/she is upset with. It is a **situation** that has caused the frustration and anger to rise above common sense.

Clients take vacations for a variety of reasons, sometimes saving up for years to afford a particular itinerary. I've learned the anticipation of departure day is somewhat overwhelming to many, wrapping up many day-to-day details in order to be gone for a period of time. In fact, the process can be very stressful. Perhaps you may have experienced this yourself.

For instance, Mr. X has promised his family this two-week cruise for over a year and his wife and children have been packing for days when he finds out the bottom has dropped out of his business world. As he is CEO and CFO (Chief Executive and Chief Financial Officer) of his company, he suddenly has to make some tough decisions. His mind is racing as he contemplates his choices: (1) call off the cruise and disappoint the family, or (2) take the attitude 'it is what it is' and put the business on hold. The cruise is paid for with hard-earned muscle and brains, it's too late for a refund and he decides to go along with the "fun family vacation."

The plane is delayed and the 'loving family' barely makes the connection, and they arrive at the ship feeling harried and pushed for time. Everyone in the family is now cranky, to say the least. It is at the moment Mr. X sees me that the pent-up little silver explosion valve on the pressure cooker is about to go off.

Here I am on this particular day, when I have arranged a meeting with clients as soon as they embark the ship, and K-Boom! Mr. X explodes. Believe me, this is more common than you might have guessed. And the same might be true at the end of the cruise when Mr. X has mentally started facing the reality of the business situation he is going home to – for a few days now his anxiety level has started to raise (big time!) and the closer he gets to disembarkation day, the silver top is primed and ready to pop off again. Sure enough it happens.

Like I indicated before, it took me years to come to terms with the fact it is not a personal thing. His pressure cooker (literally) is felt very deeply within and sooner or later he is going to explode.

Medical conditions also cause anxiety as the person affected can be stepping out of the comfort zone by leaving familiar surroundings and boarding a cruise ship. Take for instance Ms. Y who is now confined to a wheelchair and using oxygen part-time, but continues to smoke like a chimney because she feels her time is limited anyway – she may as well enjoy her habit.

Cruise ships have smoking policies everyone must adhere to, wheelchair or not, and Ms. Y comes onboard to find out she will be limited when having the luxury of feeding her long-term habit.

You get the picture, and sometimes it is not a pretty one. It's human behavior coming out in various ways. The psychology of it all can be overwhelming at times. Even though the docile personality far outweighs the pressure cooker one, certain situations still have to be addressed. How do we do that as professional Cruise Hosts? I found a secret "model."

EXERCISES

1. Can you relate to pent-up anger being directed at you?
2. What lessons have you learned in dealing with a touchy situation?
3. If you were the Cruise Host, how would you handle Mr. Y and Ms. X ?

CHAPTER 4

SECRET MODEL FOR CONFLICT CONFRONTATION

One of the toughest parts of my job is to deal with situations such as the examples in Chapter 3. Somehow these individuals feel "victimized," in my opinion, and I must face the consequences as I deal with the behavior.

Obviously there are many different "personality types" that fit the "victimized" when it comes to clientele, but in general, the steps "Mr. Victim" seems to go through are listed below (as best I can explain them).

Note: Though I use "Mr. Victim" in the reference below, it could as easily be named a "Ms. Victim" for the example.

Mr. Victim enters what I call a Conflict Confrontation Cycle because he feels victimized and responds accordingly.

1. **Victim.** Anger seems to surface when a person feels victimized in some way. Webster describes a victim as "one harmed by an act, circumstance or condition."
2. **Aggressor.** The victim enters the cycle with explosive and enraged verbal abuse and becomes an aggressor "the practice of using hostile action toward another."
3. **Martyr.** The victim/aggressor continues the cycle by expressing martyrdom "enduring great suffering."

4. Savior. The victim may feel discomfort about his behavior and feel a need to rectify the situation by offering some personal "savior" technique to feel better about himself – like giving a gift or special compliment to put the situation to rest. His offering somehow lets him off the hook in his own mind and he doesn't have to stop and analyze his own behavior or try and change it in any way.

Or at the end of this cycle the victim may **feel saved** by "running out of gas" with it all and the situation sort of fizzles out, so to speak.

The reactions might have been brought on by the feeling of victimization exclaimed as: "I'm not getting my money's worth" when a port stop is cancelled or "I'm having to wait in the airport for hours when everyone else in the group is flying out as soon as we dock."

As the Cruise Host, I have nothing to do with the circumstances, of course. I cannot control the weather or the flight schedules. Yet, I'm still in front of the group as a person to blame. And sometimes people NEED someone to blame. Mr. Victim comes at me with angry accusations that escalate into an aggressive, verbal attack.

At first I am taken off guard. Obviously I am not looking for confrontation, and it takes a moment to regain a sense of "balance" once the attack begins. Interestingly enough, when I have been traveling with a group for a period of time and begin to understand the various personalities in the group, sometimes in the back of my mind I may be aware of a possible explosion – yet when it actually does present itself, I am still taken off guard. Therein lies the psychology of it all.

I've found when I quietly allow the behavior to "run it's course" (though sometimes very hard to do), it is quite common in the uncomfortable part of the cycle Mr. Victim winds down from the anger mode and starts to look at things more logically in trying to find resolution. At other times, I feel as though I'm dodging a full round of bullets aimed directly at my face.

REACTING TO THE CONFRONTATION

Here is my secret "model" I try and live by:
- Do not get drawn into Mr. Victim's cycle of aggressive behavior in a confrontational way as two sets of anger make matters worse.

- Try using the resolution technique of 'I understand how you feel,' as that often defuses the anger and Mr. Victim doesn't quite know what to say in response.
- Assure Mr. Victim you will try to help in any way you can while not making any promises as to the outcome.
- If the behavior becomes too aggressive, tell Mr. Victim upfront you are going to walk away from the discussion until some sense of calm can be present in trying to bring about resolution. Then walk away.
- Recognizing a narcissistic personality, keep trying for a sense of calm but also be realistic in understanding there may be no solution. In his/her mind, the narcissist is **always** right.

While working for a Tour Operator, you might explain to the client you are documenting the situation in your report at the end of the cruise. From that point on, it is up to the two of them (the Tour Operator and the client) to discuss and/or resolve the problem later (if there is a cooperative solution).

In any case, you may or may not be able to bring about resolution. What is important is the fact you know you have tried to do whatever you can to rectify the situation. For me it's all about finding that inner peace that says *"I've done all I can do."*

Some of my most difficult clients who demonstrated high levels of intensity during the cruise expressed thanks at the end of the trip for my professionalism. Sometimes I walk away thinking *"thanks for the apology,"* as I know with some human beings giving a compliment is their way of apologizing. Some will never be able to say *"I'm sorry for the way I acted."* It's okay.

Others will. That's okay, too. It's important to me that I know I have acted and reacted in as kind and loving way as I can. There can be merit to the old clique *"Kill 'em with kindness."*

I have seen others in my profession react to situations in various ways. It seems however we act or react is all a part of the way in which we were raised plus whatever we have learned along the way. 'Actions speak louder than words' was coined a long time ago, but it still holds today.

Additionally various situations can demand a much stronger voice. Recently a peer of mine had a situation where a woman was draining the energy of the entire group by the way she was acting. When that happens and you cannot get the momentum turned around, a heart-to-heart talk with the individual may be inevitable.

Sometimes this is where the "listening" comes into play. As Ms. Z began telling me her life story on a recent trip, I realized she was feeling lonely and afraid as her children had deserted her years ago and now she is facing health issues. She was "taking it out on everyone else" at every gathering, and her attitude was causing dissention within the group of ladies who sat together at dinner.

Probably the reason I love the psychology part of group dynamics is it becomes a challenge to try and turn that person's attitude around. When I learned what was happening, I asked Ms. Z to stop by my hospitality desk where we could have a chat, just the two of us. That is when I learned about her lonely life and the problem of facing her fears. I suggested she try using the "replace fear with love" idea and asked her to practice with me. I told her I would interrupt her from time to time as she was facing her fears. She agreed to try it.

She would begin talking negatively, wherein I would kindly interrupt, ask her to take a deep breath and think about changing her mindset "from A (negative) to B (positive)" and tell me the story again. She ended up actually getting the idea and began practicing the positive reinforcement. By the time she left the cruise she was not only accepted in a much better way by her dining group, but also determined to try and reconnect with her children. Sometimes life's circumstances get in the way of who we are inside. Once the cocoon is cracked open, it can be a much brighter day outside.

Always the discussion needs to take place away from the group. When and if a difficult and angry situation exists (as in the case of Mr. Victim), I would suggest making copious notes about the entire set of circumstances you are dealing with – and also make a mental note of the person(s) in the group that are obviously feeling your pain in having to deal with the 'impossible person.' I've had persons write letters to the Tour Operator in my behalf or tell me they are willing to write if I need validation regarding a certain incident or incidents.

You may choose to call or e-mail the Tour Operator and make them aware of a difficult situation and ask for direction. It is always comforting to know you have support if you have to choose to make a confrontation. Of course if you are the Tour Operator, it is up to you to determine if the client is worth keeping, and act however your conscience allows.

Sometimes cruisers get spoiled because they have been longtime travelers with the same cruise line and are used to getting their own way. Or sometimes they are of the mindset they somehow *deserve* to get their own way. Cruisers can be spoiled and human beings can be difficult.

That's a given. How I handle the situation is up to me.

EXERCISES

1. How do you handle confrontational situations? Can you walk away?
2. Have you thought about your own behavior as it relates to Mr. X? How about Ms. Z?
3. How does "patience" fit into the examples used?

CHAPTER 5

USING THE SECRET "MODEL"

∾

The model came in handy when a Tour Operator abandoned me. I was responsible for 165 clients and no help when a colleague had to leave prior to departure because of a family emergency. My peer told me he had already contacted the company to inform them about the circumstances. I also informed them but did not get any answers, nor did they send a replacement for my colleague.

So, basically, that meant I alone had to meet company requirements of delivering printed materials to all the cabins, post welcomes on all cabin doors (LOTS of cabin doors), handle all client complaints, cover hospitality desk hours alone, be "Julie" at all the social events – and deal with limited crew on a failing cruise line. The cruise ship had mechanical problems, causing us to miss our first port stop, Victoria, B.C., while continuing to "limp along" on our Alaska Inside Passage cruise.

Because the cruise line's financial condition was in jeopardy at the end of the cruise, I had to work with what was left of the ship staff to re-book plane reservations and get everyone home safely. About 130 ended up laughing with me while conditions got worse. What would you guess the others acted like?

I also used the model on a cruise when the Tour Operator I worked for set up parameters that I was required to work within, but extenuating circumstances made arrangements impossible to carry out. Balancing the accusatory remarks from some, with sincere praise from others, brought about an interesting group dynamic. From that situation I learned negative energy can destroy but only if you let it. I chose to record the positives in my mind.

What's great about the model, I've found, is it can be used in interaction with family members, business associates in an office atmosphere, committee work involving church functions – you name it. Now you have your own little **secret model** to carry with you throughout life. Try it out and see if it works. Yes, it takes practice. Isn't life about learning?

EXERCISING CONTROL

One important thing I have learned is this: display confidence in your attempt to find a solution to the problem if at all possible, but never guarantee results. Let the explosion die down by explaining you are walking away to find out more details in order to help in any way you can.

As stated this model can be practiced with any relationship you are in, be it family or friends or in an office atmosphere. It can be used at your child's soccer game, in an office situation where egos are large and tempers run rampant or in a vehicle when your spouse or companion starts to confront you. Get out of the vehicle. Do not engage.

You do not have control over the person who feels victimized, but you do have control over your reaction to that person. Exercise your control.

Is this easy? No, it is a hard lesson to learn. Conditioned behavior takes practice. I can almost guarantee you will not be good at it when you start to practice the technique, especially if you were raised in an argumentative household.

What do you play in your head? **Do not engage in the cycle.** Remember YOU have a choice. You can choose to get in the cycle or choose to stay out. You are at the helm of your own cruise ship. Why not steer it toward the smooth water?

EXERCISES

1. Are you regularly confronted by the type behavior mentioned in this chapter? How do you handle it?
2. Are you willing to try the model on your cruise to self discovery?
3. Do you think the model will work for you? Why or why not?

Write down situations you recall where you were the person feeling victimized and how you handled it.

1.
2.
3.
4.

Now write down situations where you were the person being attacked and how you could have changed your own behavior.

1.
2.
3.
4.

PART V

SECRETS OF CRUISING INTO THE FUTURE

CHAPTER 1

A JOURNEY OF PEACE

∽

When looking to build the future, revisiting the past is not always a bad thing. If the waves of your last career challenge came in what seemed like tsunami force, building a stronger vessel to withstand the future tides of change may enhance your personal cruise to a perfect landing.

As the successive parts of this book started to merge and continue toward a concrete dock, I came to realize a need to share just one more story, that of my own personal journey toward enlightenment and peace while working in my perfect career of choice. I share this experience because it has, perhaps, been the most important journey of all.

'Peace' came about through my wanderlust cruise world, written in part on the decks of ocean-going cruise ships or near a riverboat paddlewheel. As I walked in the moonlight, or considered the ocean in front of me, it is here that I began to know peace – real peace. A deck is a beautiful thing in the creative process.

A Cruise Host career might also bring one into an unknown future, just as you are experiencing mine as we continue on our journey together. Tomorrow is a whole new day.

The term **career change** had never entered my mind when in January 1995, I experienced a lightning bolt signal to pack my bag and take a trip to Israel and Egypt. The idea came out of nowhere when I attended an ITMI Symposium and the speaker asked the audience to write down a dream of something we would like to do.

Life on the home front seemed anything but restful as I struggled with a sense of foreboding, loneliness, insecurity and depression. Though I couldn't quite put a finger on the reason, inner peace continued to evade me. I didn't have much of any kind of dream to get excited about. In fact, my dreams seemed lost at sea.

Since I knew a former pastor had taken some tour groups to the Holy Land, I wrote I would like to organize my own group and join Dr. Jim Farley on one of his journeys. In my mind there are no accidents – by August I had my group ready to go the following February.

It may seem strange to think about going to a war-torn area of the world in search of peace, but my vision was clear. That lightning bolt was a gift, and excitement began to build as I planned for my visit to the places I had heard and read about all my life.

In preparation for the trip, my friend Janet agreed to help make little shiny angels out of brown paper bags to present to the people on our coach. I was driving up Interstate 25 toward Ft. Collins, CO to meet her when suddenly I received the words to a poem entitled "Peace." I quickly recorded them on a yellow-lined pad on the front seat of my car, driving at 75 mph.

Though I wouldn't recommend traveling at that speed while attempting to write a poem, it was indeed a significant pivotal point in an adventure-filled journey that is long from being over. Perhaps I paved the way at the time, however, for trying to text and drive at the same time – which has since been outlawed in Colorado. Next time I might pull off the highway at least – to receive direction from the higher ups!

About the same time I entered into counseling for my confused state. I learned while experiencing a difficult time it is sometimes helpful to draw, build or make something to transition from one phase of life to another. I felt as though I had so much love to share yet everything felt off balance. I was primed for creation and waiting for a knock.

For my focused renewal I chose to build a tiny little pyramid (actually it resembled more of a triangle with three sides instead of four – what was I thinking?!), lovingly molded and constructed from a box of the girls' old modeling clay. Each color represented a period in life, starting with Joy (Blue) as a foundation and moving up with Hope (Red), Love (Yellow) and Peace (Green).

With intentional purpose, I left the green top off and used a mental challenge to place everything I didn't like about myself into the symbolic structure, then place the green top on at the Western Wall in Jerusalem and pray for peace since it felt like I had none in my life at the time.

I left the tiny multi-colored pyramid safely tucked away in a crack in the wall, as together two friends and I prayed. It seemed most appropriate Janet and Donna be there with me. I had shared with them many circumstances surrounding my situation, while assuming most all the problems I was dealing with must be my fault. Isn't it funny how we enablers allow those ideas to compound in our heads?

SURPRISE BOMBS, PHYSICAL AND MENTAL

I went on the trip with a group of thirteen from Colorado, joining with others to make up two full coaches. We all toured in Israel, and a smaller group including me continued our travels in Egypt where we visited the pyramids among other locations. While in Jerusalem, a bomb went off and shook the hotel windows where we stayed. I opened a window in my stuffy room to sounds of a bird chirping in a tree outside, while voices muted in prayer sang out from the Western Wall. A sense of stillness came over me as I marveled in the peace while in this place of unrest.

Touring that day went on without fail. Sitting at lunch by our Israeli tour guide, Yossi, I listened intently as he described all the feelings about the bombs that ravaged his soul. Among them were anger, distrust, fear, disgust, sadness, rage, heartache, hurt, anxiety and pain. Somehow his words resonated with me all the way home yet I still carried this profound sense of peace in my heart.

People at home didn't understand our experience. I couldn't experience it for them, and words were not adequate to explain how all of the above could be possible. How could anyone be at peace mentally with bombs going off in the midst of turmoil?

While reliving the situation at home, I personally found inward meaning and began writing prolific poetry. Putting into words Yossi's emotional response of that day came out in my work as I sometimes wrote 10-12 poems during the course of a day/evening/night. What became apparent was the fact I was experiencing the same feelings he expressed – in my personal quest for answers.

The poetry was a miraculous discovery of an art I had never considered before. "John Brown went to town" was the most I had ever written. I couldn't explain it nor did I try. It felt like years of my life were being recorded in time by a means totally foreign to me. And somehow the life vest of discovery gave me new energy and synergy. I felt as though my brand new cruise ship had just been christened and was ready to cast off.

To my amazement, writing poetry was a freeing process. It was as though I was spilling out emotions that had been sealed away for years in the darkness of that cocoon previously mentioned. The depth of the subject matter was profound.

Scenes from the trip reappeared in my mind often, and became a magnificent photograph of hope – scenes like standing under the Jerusalem sign as our coach waited to climb the steep hill to the city where 'all roads lead,' scenes like my minister literally jumping, laughing, crying, singing, shouting, joyfully praising as we waited for the coach to move on.

The trip itself confirmed my faith, my ability to seemingly reach out and touch the hand of God. I was re-baptized in the Jordan River and felt the intense presence of support in my state of questioning and searching for answers. I walked the Stations of the Cross with Catholic and non-Catholic friends as our tears fell in unison. We shared Communion near the location where Christ may have lain, I lathered mud on my body to take away the wrinkles (a joyous occasion but I think it failed!) while bobbing in the Dead Sea – and walked in the beauty of a Garden called Gethsemane. Generations of those before us became the carpet on which we walked. Centuries old water viaducts and ancient stone walls were walking companions.

Even in the midst of bombs going off, I never felt afraid. My mind did visit the magnitude of it all – however I was secure in feeling a sense of oneness if these were in fact my last days on this earth as we traveled in the Valley of the Shadow of Death. I actually did 'fear no evil' as certain landscapes represented uncertainty just over the hill from a field of wildflowers where the Sermon on the Mount was shared.

Geologically, historically, mentally, physically, spiritually every day was exhausting yet intensely profound in a sense of wonderment and awe. Our Jewish tour guide Yossi led us to the Holocaust Museum as our Palestinian coach driver waited – like the cooperative team they were throughout the trip.

Nothing quite compared, however, to the feeling that the location where the three crosses stood represents forgiveness. My life was forever changed in the embodiment of grace as I wrote with conviction – words that contained energy and inspiration as I revisited those four stages of life in my mind: Joy, Hope, Love and Peace.

PEACE

© CarolLee Miles 1996

Peace is so restful, it comes with God's love..
A blessed assurance, a gift from above.

Peace is a mountain her majesty reigns
Peace is a river, a dove 'ore the plains

Peace comes with breathing air deep in our chests
While watching a snowflake as gently it rests

Peace is a sunrise, it lights up the sky
Peace is a sunset, each days passes by

Peace is a moment, humans in space
Peace is God speaking HIS loving grace

Peace is a newborn tiny and frail
Peace at a distance, a ship with a sail

Peace comes not in colors like various skin
Peace comes in our hearts no matter our kin

Peace for all nations – we ask for HIS care
Peace for all ages as humbly we share

Peace is a gift, it comes from within
Peace gives us strength with God our best friend

Yes, Peace is so restful, it comes with God's love
A blessed assurance, a gift from above.

EXERCISES

1. Identify the mental and physical bombs that have gone off in your life.
2. How did or do you choose to deal with them?
3. Do you believe the end result can be a positive one?
4. How could/would that affect your career?

CHAPTER 2

A CD ENTITLED 'PEACE'

One never knows when something powerful is about to happen. For me "something powerful" somehow seems to be connected to a cruise ship, and the following secret is no exception.

August of the same year rolled around and I was on that problem-filled Alaska cruise I wrote about earlier. It had been a cruise marked with uncertainty and trials from beginning to end. Quite frankly I was ready to get off the ship and find my way home.

On the last night there was a passenger talent show, so I decided to join in some raucous fun and share a cute salmon poem that drew deep-seated laughter and applause. I followed that with an explanation of the Holy Land experience, describing the bombs going off and what it felt like at the time. I followed the story with the 'PEACE' poem I had been given, penned from the yellow-lined tablet six months earlier.

Receiving a standing ovation as I walked out and feeling pretty proud, a man named Jeff Norman grabbed my arm and said: "We need to talk." We met later and he told me the poem could easily be a National Anthem, sung by Whitney Houston or Barbra Streisand. After I realized he was indeed serious about his reaction to the poem, I stepped back and pinched myself to make sure I was in the moment and not living in a dream.

He then gave me a card for his father-in-law who has a recording studio in CA and asked me to call him in two weeks and ask him to put the poem to song. To say I was overwhelmed when someone said those things about a poem I wrote is an understatement. Talk about searching for a career? Music has always been a part of me but songwriting had never even entered a realm of possibility. Was this more than a simple nudge? Indeed it seemed like a real bolt of lightning this time. A big one!

I wasn't in on the process of recording that first song and had no idea what to expect when the tiny tape recording suddenly appeared in the mail. February seems to be a notable month for me and that's when it arrived in 1997. I couldn't stop playing it. Ted Perlman recorded it in his studio in California and his wife Peggi Blu belts out 'Peace' like there's no tomorrow. If someone had handed me $1 million, I couldn't have been more joyous. I tucked it away in a tiny cassette recorder that became my constant companion. My heart overflowed with joy.

Through a bizarre set of circumstances I was led to various musical artists around the country who continually said my words were not poems but rather song lyrics. Each time I replied, "Okay. Then make them into a song." And they did. Every set of words that became a song was a part of me. I was beginning to understand the world of songwriting and how artists turn thoughts into music as my cruise world came to life.

Over the next months Donna and I flew to CA to meet Ted, Peggi and their charming son Christopher because they somehow felt like family. I felt drawn to see his studio first-hand and later went back to experience what it's like when a song is about to go into production. Ted recorded two more songs there.

After that I spent considerable time in the Caravell Studio in Branson, MO where the entire set of musical arrangements were finally mastered by Eddie Wilson, a master of music himself. Even more important was the fact my mom and sisters were involved in much of the recording process in Branson, just three hours south of where Mom lived in our hometown of Marshall, MO. The fact they were involved made it even more special. They shared in my reverence and my calling, as well as my spontaneity and craziness.

I kept dialing my dear friend Kathy, and asking her to pray, because everything was moving so fast it seemed overwhelming at times. I had a hard time grasping the magnitude of it all. Her kitchen barstool had held my frame years earlier in times of need, allowing me to feel the comfort of that old familiar maple tree on the farm. Her voice as well as other very dear friends' voices held me up and made me strong, I am forever grateful for that support.

Yes, I did finally have the experience of putting on a set of earphones in a studio, in fact the studio of my alma mater, the University of Northern Colorado in Greeley, CO, where the last song on the CD "My Mom, My Friend" was recorded. Yes, Mom was there in Spirit, too! I'm sure of it.

Horace Lowe, Denver Attorney-at-Law, turned out to be my spiritual mentor, citing Bible verses from Scripture where he was sure I had gotten the words for poems (when I hadn't even read the scriptures). After that, believe me when I say I started reading! Dr. Gene Aitken, Professor of Jazz Studies at UNC, was the first "music expert" to listen to the 'granddaddy song PEACE' through a set of headphones in his tiny office. He laid down the headphones, smiled and said: It's Whitney Houston! Wait a minute. Wasn't she one who Jeff Norman mentioned when he heard the poem? Indeed. Gene used his own highly successful musical expertise to advise me on the journey and help with some recordings – while affirming this wild ride was all good stuff.

In six months time, we finished fifteen more recordings – from little poems in a brown folder to finished works – as our little team took on two more composers, Jed Lance and Daniel Market. I felt as though God was directing every detail as we laughed, cried and rejoiced in the final production. Two short years after what seemed like a whirlwind of "newness" and certainly a mind-boggling experience, my new CD arrived with eighteen songs set to music by four different composers around the country. I felt as though I had birthed a baby so full of joy I couldn't wait to share this beautiful experience with the world. Talk about abundance!

Here was a musical tribute to a lot of the places where I had traveled, experiences I had shared and emotions that were destined to emerge. My personal, cruise and travel life arrived – packaged in CD form. I am still amazed at the legacy I will leave the physical world, having no idea why I was chosen to hold the pen of creation.

I certainly had not planned this new "career," but I embraced the magnitude of it all while many of the songs came from the energy powers of the universe – making it all feel *connected* in some magical way to the air, earth, fire, space and water. I used those same forces for my own energy powers to open up a new connection with life itself.

I felt inspired and motivated again. Though I didn't understand it at the time, now I do. Healing, precious healing was beginning to take place.

Calls started coming with heartfelt thanks for the motivation and inspiration, and today I still remain in awe of the entire experience when someone tells me they play the CD all the time – twelve years after it's inception. It is obvious the work could only have been achieved by a power much greater than me, steering the ship. Yet I was still having a hard time navigating the dry dock in my own back yard, except for the magic of 'PEACE' that kept me going.

Dream Board! Dream Board! Dream Board! The lifeline to curious and new developments wrapped around the core of my being and precariously held fast as a new adventure was taking place. I called it dancing to a song of peace.

Remember I mentioned in Part I the connection of man, land and sea? I remain thrilled in the experience of personally making that connection in my own life's journey. Never underestimate what is in store for YOU to experience in your future. It matters not your age or stage in life. Just hold on when the life force happens. And enjoy the ride.

EXERCISES

1. Have you ever been impacted by a special event such as the talent show I participated in on the cruise ship?
2. How did it affect you?
3. Did you follow up on it? If not, why?
4. Do you dance to a song of Peace? If not I'd like to help you learn the steps.

CHAPTER 3

CHANGING LIVES

There are many things about the music that continue to encourage me and help me understand the CD is impacting people across the nation and even the world. Binh Rybacki, Founder of Children of Peace International, (www.childrenofpeace.org) took a copy to Vietnam where the music helped quiet the children in her orphanages filled with children from the streets of poverty and human slavery. Visiting one of her orphanages impacted my own life even more.

After being in Vietnam, I then carried copies of the CD to Cambodia where James and Athena Pond and children are changing and impacting lives affected by human trafficking through www.transitionsglobal.org. No matter the language, music carries each of us to another world. I left a part of me there, too.

With that in mind, I continue to give copies to any person that suggests he/she is working with orphanages or people in despair anywhere in the world. Copies have also gone to Haiti, India, several countries in Africa, Romania, Guatemala, Israel, Jordan, Iran, Mexico, Russia and the Philippines. Perhaps this book will enable it to travel even further.

It is the children of the world, including our own grandchildren, who seem to understand their own personal meaning as they select their favorite songs. Parents of children have called me to say their child has been impacted by the music. The same is true for adults from various walks of life, including our oldest daughter Traci who shared with me the ways in which it has impacted her own life. When she exclaimed "You're back!" we both knew it was (is) true.

"PEACE" has been there for all of us as we struggle through pain and look toward a new horizon. Probably the lives changed the most were those of the family closest to me. Our journey has been long and arduous, yet as I sit here writing today I am listening to the sounds of two doves on the back fence where antelope play in the distance. Every step of the way, there have been blessings too numerous to mention. What I chose (and choose) to hear is a song of peace. It makes me feel like dancing.

EXERCISES

1. Has some experience impacted your life and helped change other lives in a positive way?
2. Are you open to such a possibility?
3. What does the word peace mean to you?
4. How would you feel about giving such a "gift" away? How important is money to you?

CHAPTER 4

BUILDING A FUTURE WITH PEACE

༄

You're probably wondering why I brought up the CD – because there were no huge monetary rewards for my efforts. Like the rewards from my travel career, it is not the dollars and cents that make one know and understand the significance of profound abundance.

As for me personally, the CD changed my life. I now have a sense of self-worth that had been lost in the annals of time. It gave me self-confidence in using all the various skills I had acquired over a lifetime and the ability to know what it means to take a huge step outside my comfort zone. I've heard it said: "You don't grow until you go." It's so true.

It solidified the love that helps replace my fears. It gave me insight to the emotional depths of sadness in a failed marriage, with a creative expression of healing, understanding, wisdom and fortitude to carry on. The songs give strength and inspire me to follow my heart.

The CD enabled me to survive in the healthiest way, and I am grateful for the renewed recognition of a cross of forgiveness combined with a greater understanding of divine love. It gave me hope in the midst of darkness and joy in the light of morning. Seeing and touching the heart of humanity through music helped me establish another of my purposes on this earth, that of finding and sharing a sense of inner peace. It defined my "career" in many ways, in fact many career changes.

P – E – A – C - E

Now let's contemplate the future together. Can we control the future? No. But can we invest in the silent direction **for** the future, a future filled with a promise we are working toward our highest good, our greatest potential, our perfect career filled with love? I believe we can. Here is my **secret** as to how to proceed as it relates to your cruise toward success.

The steps are simple. And I'm sure you are very surprised my thinking involves the word **peace.** To that end first get relaxed and take a couple of deep breaths. Now take a couple more. Breathe in the thoughts listed below. Exhale after each letter and thought as you let go of fear, anxiety and doubt. Let each letter empower you with the greatness you deserve as you wrap your arms around yourself with love.

P – Pause for Peace. Identify your Passion(s).
    (Sit with that for a time while you dream.)
E – Eliminate Negative Energy. Exercise to Energize.
    (Pinpoint who or what is dragging you down.)
A – Analyze Your Actions; Adjust Your Attitude.
    (Record these and take action first in your mind.)
C – Create Your Ideal Career. Change Requires Courage.
    (Embrace these "C"s.)
E – Examine your past.
  Explore your present.
  Envision your future.
  Embrace your fortune.

Your vision is your greatest roadmap to success. A wrong turn is okay but when that feeling in your inner sense of wisdom says go the other way, a resurrection is about to take place. I've learned to be patient with the process.

Patience is a quieting of the stormy seas when the gentle waves of serenity provide a sense of calm, a respite from anxious bewilderment and an assurance all is well. Quietly affirm: *It is well with my soul.* I constantly tell myself I am *exactly* where I am supposed to be.

I take notice from my heart as it speaks very loudly when I am willing to honestly listen – I search for truth.

I allow my mind to wander as I consciously embrace inner calm, eliminating frenzy and anxiety-ridden sources of unease. Visualize an inner calling – what does it look like, feel like?

One thing I've learned is to allow my thoughts to be without confinement – or boundaries. I've learned to let my thoughts wander aimlessly and to release all fear into a universe of wholeness and goodness, a oneness for my highest potential – I do this by picturing my grandchildren in their innocence, with giggles and excitement about a colorful butterfly. Mentally I see an astronaut walking on the moon while singing the 'peace' song – then picture myself walking the Red Carpet to receive a Dove Award. There are no limits. I've learned anything is possible when looking in the mirror to reaffirm: I believe in you.

Dream board! Dream board! Dream board!

- Dream it.
- Speak it.
- Write it.
- Live it.

Love, love, **love yourself** as you mentally transition into the work you love and deserve. Then take that first step to make it happen.

I was just starting to take my first steps when I met Tama Kieves at a women's empowerment seminar. She inspired me to read her book: "This Time I Dance! Creating the Work You Love" that describes becoming a Harvard Law School honors graduate and very successful attorney. She then (in her words) "left it all to have it all." She kept asking herself, "If you're this successful doing work you **don't** love, what could you do with work you **do** love?" It made sense.

To me life is a never-ending pathway to discovery. At that point in life I was searching for new ways of thinking and rationalizing while carrying around my brand new CD and wondering what was next. I remember thrusting it in Tama's hands and saying, "I'm supposed to give this to you because one day I'm sure we will be working together, walking the same path or dancing to the same music." She joyously giggled and we embraced a new friendship. In friendships there is learning.

Tama taught me many things in her book and self-discovery classes. It's no wonder she's a sought-after speaker and success coach — you can check out her many resources at www.AwakeningArtistry.com. She confirmed that *inner voice* of direction and truth I experienced with the CD. And she also confirmed finding work you **do** love is a wonderful way to live your life — a roadmap to your highest good — a pathway filled with light and understanding.

Determining the direction for your future will allow a business plan to come into focus, or at least start the wheels turning as you direct your thoughts. The wildest of dreams can come true.

EXERCISES

1. When was the last time you paused for peace in your life to look into your future?
2. Can you relate to the 5 steps? Are you ready to USE them?
3. Are you willing to "leave it all to have it all"?
4. Why or why not?
5. Do you have a goal-setting plan? Are you using it?

CHAPTER 5

WRITING MY SONG/SINGING YOURS

Every time I am called to Cruise Host, or find another training that allows me to explore the seas, my suitcase is ready to go as I continue to write my own songs. Yes, I continue to envision myself in a perfect place, at a perfect time, on that perfect itinerary. Who knows? Perhaps I'll take an Around the World Voyage one day. It's on my Dream Board.

My last two-week Hawaii cruise was a little rocky, but it was the perfect place to examine the past, explore the present, and envision the future.

I've been called about several Cruise Host possibilities in the near future that all look promising from a work standpoint – the economy seems better in that regard. Meanwhile I embrace the fact my recent 'down time' was meant for writing a new melody through literary channels – while that old familiar song of peace still rings in my ear and keeps me polishing my dance shoes for the next tango at sea.

I also continue to educate myself, and work at growing www.CLMPeaceTravel.com to find more places for recess rather than w-o-r-k. Cruising, my first love, will continue to grow through hard effort and determination. On the horizon you might look for some group cruises offered using Part I for training – a real, hands-on experience of Cruise Hosting.

Want to join me as together we cast off into the sunset? If so, go to www.CarolLeeMiles.com/Training and check out the possibilities. Also send me your suggestions. I promise to check them out as well.

ROWING THE BOAT TO FREEDOM

Though rowing a tiny lifeboat to safety was tough going, and hard to maneuver through extremely rough waters, the rewards have already been limitless. I have grown in ways I could not have imagined possible while stepping out into a lonely world – supported by the constant reassurance of sustainable and unquestionable faith. Yes, I still have my Bible with the heart on it. One thing is certain. Pen and paper will never be very far away. Faith and love are also close at hand.

Freedom will continue to define my journey. Perhaps it will help you define your own future as you begin to think about writing your own song. I truly hope so. Do you have a melody in mind? If not, just write down some words on a yellow-lined notebook. It worked for me.

One last thing you may want to consider: If you are happy and content with that joy, joy, joy, joy down in your heart, I encourage you to stay the course and not rock the boat. When the time is right perhaps you will see another cruise ship off in the distance and decide to chart new waters. Until that time, smooth sailing is always a good thing. I highly recommend it. Grab onto the bow and sing to your heart's content.

EXERCISES

1. What have you done with your life? Where are you now?
2. How would you use the chapters in this book to help fulfill your dreams?
3. Does freedom define your journey? If not, what does?

CHAPTER 6

THE SECRET OF YOUR SUCCESS

༄

In the quiet you will find answers. Go there and listen. It may indeed be found in the apron you are wearing as you prepare the next meal for your family, or your professional hat that fits you in your business world today.

If it's Julie on Love Boat you want to pursue, I can attest to the fact your life will be filled with both smooth and rough waters, but that's okay. You may come out leaving the life vest behind as you walk on solid ground.

Wherever you are in life, may the smooth waters of love and understanding nurture and sustain.

As you miraculously write to the music of your own soul, you will find it gets easier to spread your wings and soar. You may even feel you have orchestrated an entire symphony, playing loud and clear while feeling the waters of experience guide you into a safe port somewhere in the distance.

May you write your own *secret* song filled with inner *peace* that sustains you for the rest of your successful career, and may God Bless you in your journey.

EXERCISES

1. Do you feel you are successful? Why or why not?
2. What is the secret of your success?
3. Are you content with your life's "song" or would you like to write a new one? Why?
4. Are you fulfilling your highest good? If not, Dream it! Speak it! Write it! Live it!

SUMMARY

This book contains personal, professional and philosophical *secrets* that will help you embark on your own successful career in the travel industry. I take you through an example cruise, give ideas for getting paid to cruise, and offer two case studies and some personal interviews. I also offer my own personal story as an example of someone who found a wonderful and successful career, defined in numerous ways.

This book also contains ideas about the psychology of working with groups, including a personal model I use during conflict confrontation. The model is easily applicable to any situation in life, as is the way I suggest you learn how to begin to replace F-E-A-R with L-O-V-E. The interactive question and answer sessions after every chapter allow you to zero in – and focus on – moving in a positive direction toward finding your perfect career in today's marketplace.

Who doesn't want to cruise into the future using peaceful means? My personal journey of peace goes far beyond the scope of imagination and theory. By sharing my secrets and wisdom accumulated over years of personal and professional travel experience, my hope is that you'll be abundantly blessed with new knowledge to use and share with family, friends and co-workers in your ideal career.
Dream it! Speak it! Write it! Live it!

HELPFUL RESOURCES

Valuable resources are available in today's technological world. Some are free and others are not. I don't want to overwhelm you with choices, but the following list may serve as a beginning for your own helpful resources list.

    CRUISE LINES INTERNATIONAL ASSOCIATION (CLIA) – CLIA is the world's largest cruise association and is dedicated to the promotion and growth of the cruise industry. CLIA is composed of 26 of the major cruise lines serving North America and provides support, trainings and certifications for travel agents. CLIA's annual 'cruise3sixty' event is powerful. www.cruising.org

    E-CAMPUS TRAVEL TRAINING PROGRAM (through YTB International, Inc.) -- A web-based, 10-course program developed by Dr. Marc Mancini who is a highly respected name in the travel world. Dr. Mancini is a sought-after speaker, educator and consultant whose books are readily available online.

    ERRORS AND OMISSIONS INSURANCE (E&O) – For those wishing to obtain personal E&O insurance, a representative of Berkely Insurance Agency was available at the last ITMI Symposium in Atlanta, GA. www.berkely.com

    Applications for phones and/or electronic devices such as Maps, Metro info, etc.

    Videos & Brochures from Cruise Lines

    Internet "travel families" on various social networks like Facebook, Twitter, etc.

BLOGS on travel/cruising; people who cruise often; old ship daily newspapers

Travel magazines (numerous are in hard copy or online)

Book Stores and Public Libraries (Travel Section and/or Cruise Section)

Tourist Bureaus, Convention and Business Bureaus, Chambers of Commerce, Foreign Government Tourist Offices (Google area interested in.)

Tourist Information Centers for brochures & info (often located near cruise dock)

Culturegrams www.culturegrams.com

Weissmann Reports www.weissmann.com

To purchase CD, go to Carolleemiles.com.
A portion of all sales will be donated to non-profits working to end human suffering.

Here are two non-profits close to my heart:

Children of Peace International
P. O. Box 2911
Loveland, CO 80539-2911
970-667-3716
www.childrenofpeace.org

Transitions Global
P. O. Box 30157
Cincinnati, OH 45230
513-898-9372
www.transitionsglobal.org

ABOUT THE AUTHOR

CarolLee Miles is a woman who lives to travel – and travels to live. Her motto is: *Dream it! Speak it! Write it! Live it!* And that's what she's done with her second creative endeavor, "Getting Paid to Cruise: Secrets of a Professional Cruise Host."

Hired by Ports of Call Travel Club in Denver, Colorado in 1986, her childhood dreams of traveling the world came true. By 1990 she had stepped foot on all 7 continents and developed an insatiable appetite for cruising and helping others, which she has done for over 25 years.

In 1993, Miles became a certified Tour Director/Cruise Host through the International Tour Management Institute, San Francisco, CA. In 1999 she became Executive Producer of a CD entitled "Peace" and received recognition for her peace work from Columbia College, Columbia, MO where she attended and her alma mater, the University of Northern Colorado.

She is currently training professional Cruise Hosts on various cruise lines and combining all aspects of her career in public speaking engagements.

Miles' motto flows throughout her journeys, including the relationship she has with her four grandchildren and their parents. By becoming an author and sharing her knowledge, she is living her dreams. CarolLeeMiles lives in the Denver area and can be reached at www.CarolLeeMiles.com.